Staff Development/ Organization Development

**Prepared by the ASCD
1981 Yearbook Committee**

**Betty Dillon-Peterson,
Chairperson and Editor**

Association for Supervision and Curriculum Development
225 N. Washington St., Alexandria, Virginia 22314

Editing:
Ronald S. Brandt, ASCD Executive Editor
Nancy Olson, Senior Editor

Cover Design:
Amy Rupp, Art Director

Stock Number: 610-81232
Library of Congress Catalog Card Number: 80-70653
ISBN 0-87120-104-6

Contents

Foreword

Barbara D. Day

ASCD HAS TRADITIONALLY ATTEMPTED, through its Yearbook, to address the most important—indeed, the most compelling—issues in education. Today, we can all agree that staff development is such an issue, one that affects those in educational leadership positions as perhaps no other issue will.

Change and growth are endemic in our complex modern society; the school or staff which does not change and grow is destined to atrophy, to become obsolete, and to be a burden rather than a bulwark to us and to the communities we serve. This is particularly true in view of the increasing pressure put on our institutions by the upward expansion of the whole learning cycle.

As the authors of this volume point out, we can no longer consider an individual's education complete after 12 to 14 years of formal schooling. Learning and growth take place throughout an individual's lifetime and must continually be a renewing process. Therefore we must deal with organizational growth and with staff development that will adequately serve both the organization and the individual. In short, we and the institutions which serve us must be self-renewing.

This requirement for self-renewal comes in a climate where teachers are apprehensive about the process of evaluation, distrustful of accountability, and fearful that they will become the scapegoat for innovations that didn't work and about which they were unexcited in the first place. In addition, our society gives high priority to tangible things—new buildings, for example—and is generally uninterested in the intangibles—staff development. Success in this climate will not be easy.

Still, we must persevere, and the writers and thinkers whose work is collected here are determined to develop a comprehensive process that will bring about self-analysis and help us achieve the renewal we seek. They are agreed that a workshop or lecture occurring at the end of a busy school day and typically covering a new curriculum emphasis does not constitute good staff development.

Included here are suggested models for staff development, programs designed to give practitioners help in providing necessary organizational and staff renewal, and suggestions for implementing the needed evaluation components. The Yearbook treats organization development as an emerging discipline that is inextricably interwoven with staff development and that contributes immeasurably to the complexity of this topic.

As noted in the introduction to Chapter 4: "The work ahead of us is to build flowing systems of staff development which help educators enrich their lives and competence, faculties improve their schools, and school systems initiate curricular and organizational changes. Until *systems* of staff development are pervasive, implementing *ad hoc* programs will be the norm." Put another way, staff development will all too often consist of meaningless lectures or workshops at the end of a busy school day until we in leadership positions adopt and promote the concepts presented in this Yearbook and accept the philosophy it promulgates.

Therein lies the real challenge.

BARBARA D. DAY
ASCD President, 1980-81

1

Staff Development/Organization Development—Perspective 1981

Betty Dillon-Peterson

THERE WAS A TIME when society seemed to change very little. Institutions and value systems were relatively stable, clearly understood, and commonly supported throughout communities. Authority was respected. Individuals seldom questioned, probed, or criticized. They stayed in one place and expected their children to do the same. Attending school was an opportunity and a privilege. Teachers taught curriculum designed for the average student and those who did not succeed were expected to find other, more suitable endeavors.

To the harried educator of today, that time may sound like a Golden Age, although perhaps it only appears so compared with today's complexity. In any case, it *is* true that we now live in a diverse world where there is little commonality of purpose, much disenchantment with public institutions, and high expectations for individual fulfillment. In the light of these circumstances, schools are scrutinized as never before. Educators are pressured from every direction to perform their primary function—teaching the basics—better. In addition, they are expected to expand the curriculum to provide for more and more of the physical, personal, and social needs of all students, while subject to steadily declining resources. In order to survive they must not become static; they *must* develop workable strategies for continuous self-renewal.

Unfortunately, little systematic attention has been given to the identification of reliable means by which schools can, in fact, become self-renewing. During education's decade of innovation—the 60s—two major forces encouraged the plethora of changes (many of which are now perceived as worthless or no longer exist). The first was the educators' and the public's awakening awareness that schools were not adequately serving the needs of all students, particularly the disadvantaged. The second force was less clearly articulated. Innovation was "in." There was a lively excitement and acceptance of the idea of trying new things in the nation's classrooms. Many changes were made, often introduced in an ad hoc manner, with little other rationale than that it "felt right."

All this activity resulted in one of the most stimulating, challenging, creative, liberating, and confusing climates in which schools and teachers had ever operated. Unfortunately, there were often no sound conceptual bases for the changes made, and the criticism of "change for change's sake" was, in many cases, well-deserved. With lack of clear purpose and dedication to the innovation, most change efforts were abandoned as reactionary forces demanded an accounting or a return to more traditional ways of doing business.

The present climate militates against personal excellence in subtle ways. Many teachers are apprehensive about evaluation of their performance. It is difficult to keep the evaluation process growth-oriented and risk-taking rather than protective and defensive. Most teachers spend their professional lives in relative isolation, both psychological and material, with little opportunity to learn from each other. Doing an excellent job brings few formal rewards.

Psychological and economic commitment to the professional growth of educators generally is a low public priority. One small school district recently paid an enormous fee to an architect to prepare plans for a vocational high school, which the Board then decided not to build. Even in this conservative community, there was little grumbling about the loss of the architect's fee, which was more than the district would spend on staff development in 100 years at its present rate of commitment. This graphically demonstrates the problem of priorities schools face as they try to convince not only staff members but also the public that staff development is important, if not crucial.

Against this backdrop of uncertainty on the part of educators and lack of confidence on the part of the public, determined, optimistic educators are working to improve schools and release the potential of the people who work in them. Their goal is to develop a coherent, comprehensive process for self-analysis and renewal. One teacher, when encouraged to attend a staff development activity, said, "I already know how to teach better than I do." Staff development's task is to make it expected that teachers will not only teach as *well* as they know how but also that they will learn more about their field while applying those learnings effectively.

Staff Development/Organization Development = Planned Change

Staff development and organization development are a gestalt of school improvement; both are necessary for maximum growth and effective change. They are complementary human processes, inextricably interwoven, dynamic, interactive, nonlinear, and incredibly complex. In order to deal with this complexity, the authors of this yearbook have provided numerous examples and models. The following definitions underlie their work:

- *Staff Development:* Staff development is a process designed to foster personal and professional growth for individuals within a respectful, supportive, positive organizational climate having as its ultimate aim better learning for students and continuous, responsible self-renewal for educators and schools.

- *Organization Development:* Organization development is the process undertaken by an organization, or part of an organization, to define and meet changing self-improvement objectives, while making it possible for the individuals in the organization to meet their personal and professional objectives.

The interrelationship between these two definitions is clear. The successful teacher is, and will remain, a key to successful learning for students. But the efforts of one person—however diligent—can be helped or hindered significantly by the environment in which he or she works. And the influence of that environment can be enhanced by helping the total organization or subsystem (school, department, team) be self-critiquing and continuously improving.

Seldom are individual development and institutional development or change discrete entities, even though they are often viewed that way. Rather, they are dependent correlates. Without one or the other—or if they operate in isolation—the potential for significant, positive change is materially decreased. Organizations are successful in fulfilling their missions only to the degree that the individuals within them understand and contribute to the achievement of mutually-acceptable goals.

Although staff development and organization development are perceived as correlates, sometimes blurring or overlapping, it may be advisable to discuss the current level of practice or knowledge about each process as background for the chapters of this yearbook.

Staff Development

Staff development is considered here by answering four questions: For whom is staff development intended? How are needs determined? How are programs designed and implemented? How are staff development efforts evaluated?

For whom is staff development intended?

Ideally, staff development is a process used to provide learning opportunities for *all* people working in schools or responsible for them. In fact, a growing number of school districts do provide staff development on a somewhat systematic basis for everyone connected with a district, including the board and superintendent, administrators, teachers, and classified personnel such as cooks, custodians, and bus drivers. In practice, most inservice training is targeted at the individual teacher, to improve the delivery of services to students. It is assumed there will be an impact on student learning, but this impact is not usually specified or measured.

How are needs determined?

Needs assessments customarily take three forms:

1. Persons in supervisory positions determine needs from their assessment of the quality of work being performed by those reporting to them.

2. Individuals are asked to state their own perceived needs or to respond to a checklist or similar instrument.

3. Groups of individuals (teams, departments, schools) respond to various internal or external pressures by planning collaboratively to bring about specific changes.

Within a given school district, all three processes may operate. Each has strengths and weaknesses. The first, more commonly applied to classified personnel, has the advantage of providing what could be a broader, more comprehensive and perhaps less subjective framework because individuals vary a great deal in their abilities to assess their own needs. However, most individuals, and particularly teachers and administrators, feel that their autonomy and professional judgment have been abridged if someone else, even in a superordinate position, diagnoses and prescribes for them. And, the ability of the superordinate to make a judgment is sometimes suspect.

The second form of needs assessment is applied most frequently to professional personnel, such as teachers and administrators. It allows almost complete autonomy on the part of those for whom the program is designed, but provides little in the way of objective, outside input.

The third form, supported by research on change, builds on the idea that individuals are more committed to carrying out plans which they feel reflect a genuine need and which they have helped to develop (Berman and Pauly, 1975, pp. 82-85). It has the disadvantage of being dependent on the effectiveness of the group process which facilitates or retards it.

A combination of these three forms of needs assessment is probably desirable in the absence of more rigorous, data-based techniques. One example of a more sophisticated approach, used in industry and now receiving some attention in education, is the assessment center. In this process, individuals are placed in simulated situations which give them an opportunity to demonstrate skills determined to be necessary for quality performance in their particular roles. Results of this kind of assessment could provide an individual staff development plan based on a profile of needs. Obviously, the selection of the skills to be assessed and the development of appropriate assessment exercises to measure those skills are difficult problems not yet satisfactorily solved.

How are programs designed and implemented?

Much more is known about how learning takes place than is used in practice. There is no effective network for communicating research findings to practitioners so that they may use these findings in a consistent way which has the cumulative effect of improving education for students. Most school districts are just beginning to collect information systematically which can be used to program for both student and staff learning needs. Only recently has serious attention been given to the specific learning styles and characteristics of adults.

In the absence of a sound data base upon which to determine needs, staff developers tend to employ a variety of relatively simplistic staff development techniques to respond to current pressures for school improvement. Typical of these "instant solutions" to long-term problems are: crash training courses in new teaching techniques, cursory introduction of new "teacher proof" curriculum materials, sensitivity training sessions prior to court-ordered desegregation, brief workshops on new state or federal regulations. These may involve an occasional inservice day with little or no follow-up, college-type courses, or large group presentations by an outside consultant.

Inservice is individualized most frequently by permitting staff members to choose the staff development activities in which they want to participate. The norm for staff development is the leader-directed lecture presentation. Seldom are small, problem-solving groups formed, and even less frequently are individuals helped to determine their own needs and given on-the-job support through coaching until skills are incorporated naturally.

How are results measured?

Evaluation of staff development efforts is primarily based on the opinions of participants, and success rests on whether they enjoyed the activity and whether it was perceived by them to be helpful. Learning objectives—as difficult to set for adults as for children—are often not made clear enough to be measurable. And if there is an attempt to be explicit, the staff development leader may be tempted to select an unimportant outcome which can be measured easily, as opposed to a more significant outcome difficult to assess. More and more, those responsible for staff development are attempting to be clearer about expected results with the intent of measuring them more competently.

Organization Development

Although organization development has been used in industry for the past 20 years, it has only recently received attention for its utility in education. In fact, recognition of its applicability to school change and renewal has come about in many cases as a result of the employment of some of its strategies by staff development leaders in an intuitive, almost accidental, way. A pragmatic analysis of what did and did not work in staff development led these staff developers to see that substantial change in the individual seldom occurs unless some kind of group process provides for support, exchange of ideas, maintenance of enthusiasm, and problem-solving capabilities. The function of organization development is to promote the effectiveness of the organization in ways which are parallel to or include those adopted by staff development to improve the effectiveness and satisfaction of individuals. Consequently, many staff development personnel consciously began to take into account the organization's function and characteristics as well as those of the individual in providing appropriate learning experiences.

The basic assumptions made by practitioners about organization development are: (1) maximum productivity and personal satisfaction are dependent on change in both the individual and the organization, and (2) there are processes which can be adopted or incorporated which will provide for positive growth in both.

Although the concepts underlying organization development are receiving more and more attention and use by practitioners, there is as yet no comprehensive, definitive research base or universally accepted organization development theory which demonstrates beyond doubt that it is a viable process for improving schools. Experts disagree about whether organization development change efforts are appropriate for schools at all; to what degree organizations can actually be equally concerned about task accomplishment and human fulfillment; whether organization development is based on a legitimate theory; and even whether or not it is a fad (Kahn, 1974).

These concerns are relatively unimportant if organization development is perceived primarily as long-range organizational improvement in problem solving, communication, collaboration, participation, trust, and uncovering and confronting conflict (Fullan, Miles, and Taylor, 1980) — skills which should be helpful in any field of collective human endeavor. Organization development does appear to provide direction in these areas, and the authors of this yearbook believe that it has significant potential if appropriately used.

There is *general* agreement that there are two purposes for organization development: to make the organization more effective in accomplishing its task and to improve the quality of life for those who work in it. There is also general agreement about what its goals should be, with the following list being representative:

1. Develop clear communication through new communications skills and new procedures for more open communication.

2. Build trust and increase understanding by opening close, personal communications so that hidden agendas and covert feelings can be dealt with in a climate of openness and authenticity.

3. Involve more people in decision making by encouraging information sharing and the identification of related responsibilities.

4. Create an open, problem-solving climate by helping companion groups to identify more clearly the problems confronting them and to develop collaborative, workable plans for solving them.

5. Increase group effectiveness by helping members analyze and improve the procedures for carrying out group tasks.

6. Uncover conflict by providing participants with procedures that allow conflict to emerge (Schmuck, 1975, p. 11).

Successful, authentic organization development efforts in schools appear to require these conditions:

1. Long-term (three-five year) commitment to an effort involving the total system or subsystem.

2. Careful passage through three phases, each of which may be subdivided and which may overlap. These phases are: entry or start-up, initial operation, and maintenance or institutionalization. Success in each of these stages is necessary for successful organization development, with the first being absolutely critical.

3. Top management and central office commitment and *actual involvement*.

4. Commitment and *involvement* of the building principal, particularly when the effort is directed at a school.

5. Use of an outside consultant whose purpose is to assist those in the system or subsystem to learn to use the components of the organization development process and to work in-depth with some staff members so they can provide their own continuing in-house leadership.

6. Voluntary commitment of a significant percentage of the individuals within the system or subsystem utilizing the organization development process, that is, all or at least a majority of the staff within a building, and perhaps parents or even students.

7. Careful planning which results in early, visible success related directly to on-the-job concerns of those who are involved in the program improvement effort they have collaboratively decided upon.

8. Provision of a modest amount of local funding, primarily to be expended on the services of the outside consultant and time for all others involved in the activity. (Research has shown that organization development efforts which have been totally or heavily funded from outside tend to disappear when that monetary incentive is gone.)

9. Incorporation of organization development strategies which become a regular way of doing business, an integral part of the self-renewing effort of a school or district, rather than something apart (Fullan, Miles, and Taylor, 1980).

Those who have worked in staff development will readily see parallels between these indicators of successful organization development and similar characteristics of effective staff development:

1. Long-term commitment to a particular direction or program, enabling the learner to proceed in an orderly way from orientation through in-depth exposure to integrated practice.

2. Meaningful involvement of those who are to be "developed" in needs assessment and planning.

3. Active participation as well as verbal commitment of key central office administrators and principals to the staff development effort.

4. Development of an in-house cadre of knowledgeable leaders who can carry on the training once the expert has departed.

5. Sufficient numbers of staff members voluntarily involved in the learning to provide an adequate support system to maintain the change long enough for it to be institutionalized.

6. Inclusion of immediate application possibilities in the training program.

7. Adequate economic support—particularly to provide time for the sustained effort needed.

The similarity of these two sets of critical characteristics appears to reinforce the notion that staff development and organization development should not be treated as separate entities. Rather they should be dealt with together so that the strategies employed in one context can be transferred to the other when appropriate.

Organization of the Yearbook

Against this background, yearbook authors and committee members have endeavored to develop a coherent, interrelated publication designed to give practitioners practical help in providing more meaningful learning for adults.

A brief overview of the chapters may help the reader see how they are related.

Chapter 2 deals with the learner as an individual and as an adult. Essentially, adult learners vary in important ways. They prefer differing levels of structure, task complexity, attention to personal needs, feedback about performance, and risk-taking.

Chapter 3 views organization development as an emergent discipline that provides concepts and skills for improving the climate and problem-solving ability of organizations. Applied to education, its goal is to help members of school organizations (faculties, administrators, community members) develop communities which effectively solve problems, initiate needed changes, and provide support for their members.

Chapter 4 describes a staff development effort which is compatible with organization development principles. Fred Wood, Steven Thompson, and Sister Frances Russell approach the problem of designing staff development systems. They provide a statement of beliefs or assumptions, present a five-stage process for creating and initiating inservice systems, and give examples of the operation of their process in schools.

In Chapter 5, Daniel Duke and Lyn Corno summarize basic evaluation theory and apply it to a staff development project, which also is compatible with organization development principles. They deal with a wide range of areas from political decisions (who will evaluate how and why; to whom and how will results be communicated?), to assumptions and procedures for evaluations.

Bruce Joyce describes a staff development scenario for the future in Chapter 6. This scenario is not startlingly different from what is present in many quality school systems today. What is important about it, perhaps, is that it is *not* startlingly different or unusual, but that it reflects a healthy and natural institutionalization of growth and improvement. It points toward the time when the teacher—and all others who work in schools—will routinely recognize the need to grow and change, will do so without a great deal of fuss, and will have a genuine feeling of satisfaction in the process.

In the descriptive language of an ASCD yearbook of nearly two decades ago, we hope that this yearbook will help us to *perceive* more clearly what individual and organizational needs may be, to *behave* in more sophisticated ways to provide more adequate educational responses to those needs, and to enable all of us and our students to *become* more nearly what we can become in terms of fulfilling our vital societal role. That is the challenge of growth and development, both for the individual and the organization.

REFERENCES

Berman, P., and Pauly, E. W. *Federal Programs Supporting Educational Change, Vol. II, Factors Affecting Change Agent Projects*. Washington, D.C.: U.S. Office of Education, Department of Health, Education, and Welfare, April 1975.

Fullan, M.; Miles, M.; and Taylor, G. "Organizational Development in Schools: The State of the Art." *Review of Educational Research* 50 (Spring 1980) : 125.

Kahn, R. L. "Organizational Development: Some Problems and Proposals." *Journal of Applied Behavioral Science* 10,4 (1974) : 485-502.

Schmuck, R.; Murray, D.; Smith, M.; Schwartz, M.; and Runkel, M. *Consultation for Innovative Schools: OD for Multiunit Structure*. Eugene, Oreg.: Centre for Educational Policy and Management, 1975.

2

Staff Development—Change in the Individual
Richard H. Bents and Kenneth R. Howey

ADULT LEARNERS DIFFER in important ways. They react differently to educational environments, perferring various levels of structure, task complexity, attention to personal needs, feedback about performance, and risk-taking.

Kenneth Howey, Richard Bents, Toni Santmire, Gene Hall, and Gordon Klopf have identified several frameworks which can be used to understand individual differences and adapt staff development environments so that human variety will be capitalized on and made productive, expanding the reach of each adult learner. They emphasize Hunt's finding that adult learning styles are not fixed. Adults change and, most important, enlarge the range of environments in which they can work comfortably.

The authors make extensive use of Hunt's applications of conceptual systems theory (which he developed with Harvey and Schroder) and summarize the principles he has developed after extensive research with teachers, parents, and children. They also draw on the formulations by Loevinger, Klopf, and Hall to weave the most comprehensive framework yet presented to guide staff development from an "adult learning styles" perspective.

Their framework is theoretically grounded and eminently practical both for broad program design and as a basis for the inservice education of staff developers who would understand their clients and how preferred learning modalities can be adapted to and enlarged.

IN A RECENT, relatively large study of staff development practices, teachers, teacher educators, staff developers, administrators, and parents of school-age students were surveyed in various parts of the country regarding their views on inservice education. While a little more than a quarter of all types of respondents believed staff development practices were generally

Also contributing to this chapter: GENE E. HALL, *Division Coordinator, Research and Development Center for Teacher Education, The University of Texas, Austin*; GORDON J. KLOPF, *Provost and Dean, Bank Street College, New York, New York*; TONI E. SANTMIRE, *Associate Professor of Educational Psychology and Measurements, University of Nebraska, Lincoln.*

of desired quality, over 40 percent perceived present practice as only fair and nearly another 30 percent indicated that inservice was in poor condition. Inservice activities for the new teacher during the critical first teaching assignment were especially lacking but teachers reported that problems persisted throughout their teaching careers (Yarger, Howey, and Joyce, 1980).

The most common form of staff development identified was the workshop or lecture, typically occurring at the end of the working day and and at a site other than the school. Staff development generally took place in a group setting with minimal accommodation to individual differences.

The data did suggest increases in surveys of teacher "needs." However, these inventories or diagnoses were at a remote and general level. Needs were often identified in terms of a curriculum emphasis (for example, environmental education) or instructional concern (for example, classroom management) teachers appeared most interested in. Specific personal/professional concerns or organization issues were seldom identified or given adequate attention. Analysis and documentation of classroom practices were also exceedingly rare.

The findings of this study corroborate other research and common perceptions. Inservice education or staff development is still frequently characterized by a late afternoon lecture-discussion on a topic of general interest. Planned linkages with the individual teacher's personal/professional perspectives and predispositions are uncommon and follow-up in specific classrooms is rare.

The importance of systematically including our knowledge of how adults grow and learn in plans for staff development programs is readily apparent. Yet, as indicated earlier, there is considerable evidence that we ignore much of what we do know. We give insufficient attention to the distinctive qualities of adult learning—how adults learn, how they prefer to learn, and what they want to learn.

Many have assumed that human development is complete by the end of adolescence. In the cognitive area, for example, Inhelder and Piaget (1958) described the change from concrete operational thinking to formal operational thinking as taking place in early adolescence. Since formal operational thought is the last stage of Piagetian theory, some assumed that formal operational thinking was attained by the end of adolescence and that no further changes in cognitive development occurred in adulthood. Research has also indicated that cognitive development is related to development in interpersonal competence (Flavell and others, 1968; Kuhn and others, 1971; Selman, 1971; Tomlinson-Keasy and Keasy, 1974), which suggested that interpersonal characteristics were also basically stabilized in adolescence.

Over the past ten years, however, evidence has accumulated which indicates that development is considerably more complex than previously thought. Current research clearly suggests that there are differences in adult learners on developmental variables in areas of cognition or ways of thinking as well as in interpersonal orientation. It has also been documented that these developmental differences account for differences in the performance of *teachers*. In the following discussion, we will review some of the common developmental differences existing in adult learners and briefly discuss the implications of these differences for the content, organization, and delivery of staff development programs.

Overview of Adult Education

Insights into adult development are helpful to those planning and providing staff development. As an individual moves through life from infancy to old age, changes are constantly taking place within the person as well as within the range of settings in which he or she lives and works. This is particularly true of teachers and administrators, because they are responsible for assisting others to succeed in a rapidly changing world.

While adult development is by no means a fully articulated concept, there has recently been an increasing amount of information generated about adults and how they learn. Systematic conceptions of adult development are now evolving. Study of adults can be traced to Sigmund Freud, with Carl Jung also making early contributions to the literature. Erik Erikson has had an enormous influence on many scholars today, particularly with his social-psychological studies of adults. Berrin, Neugarten, Kohlberg, Hunt, Loevinger, Heath, Chickering, Sprinthall, and Selman have been engaged in research on adults for several years now, and second and third generation scholars are following them.

Chickering (1974) divided adult developmental theorists into two basic groups: developmental *age* theorists and developmental *stage* theorists. Theorists tend to develop concepts and systems or relationships consistent with their own orientation. A psychologist's perceptions of adults will differ from those of a sociologist or a biologist. We will address both age-related and stage-related concepts here. However, since the focus of this chapter is on the individual, our discussion will rely primarily on those concepts developed from a psychological perspective. Sociological perspectives are presented more fully in Chapter 3 on Organization Development.

Both age and stage are elusive concepts and call for definition. Age theorists are interested in determining if there are concerns, problems, and tasks which are common to most or all adults at various times in their lives. They are also concerned with explaining *why* certain concerns, problems, and tasks might loom more prominently at one time of life than at another and how these affect adult behavior. Berrin, Levinson, Gould, and Sheehy are among age theorists who discuss adult development in such terms as life periods, passages, stages of life, and periods of transition.

Stage theorists, on the other hand, focus on distinct or qualitative differences in the structure of thinking (modes of thinking) at various points in development that are not necessarily age-related. The different structures or ways of thinking form an invariant sequence or progression in individual development. These structural changes provide insight into what information an individual tends to use, how that information is used, and the type of interactions he or she might have with the environment.

Studies, especially those concerned with the way people typically learn in schools, point to distinct personal traits that predict success as an adult. The names for these traits vary from the familiar to the esoteric, for example, ego maturity, psychological maturity, personal competence, allocentrism, integrity, role-taking ability, accurate empathy, symbolic processing, interpersonal competence; nonetheless, they are all highly similar (Sprinthall and Sprinthall, 1980). They all underscore the importance of cognitive-developmental structures as significant determinants of life performance. Piaget, Kohlberg, Hunt, Sprinthall, Loevinger, and Perry are among the stage theorists who view adult development in a definite progression from concrete, undifferentiating, simple, structured individuals to more abstract, differentiating, complex, autonomous yet interdependent individuals.

We should add that the distinction between age and stage theorists is not totally discrete or even as discrete as the preceding paragraphs might suggest. Rather, age is the major variable for some theorists whereas the structure of thinking is the major variable for others. Cross fertilization of ideas has occurred between these theorists and will continue as the body of knowledge regarding adult development is enlarged. For example, while Kohlberg has carefully refrained from relating a developmental stage to a specific chronological age range, he has acknowledged that his data indicate that no adults have reached his two highest stages of moral development before ages 23 and 30 respectively.

In summary, the cruciality of considering adult development relative to inservice or staff development might best be illustrated by the work of David Hunt. The most comprehensive set of studies regarding adult *teachers* has been undertaken by this developmental psychologist/educator and his associates at the Ontario Institute for Studies in Education. Hunt has been able to document through research in natural settings that teachers who were assessed at more advanced developmental stages (conceptual level) were viewed as more effective as classroom teachers in several ways. For example, teachers at higher stages of development functioned in the classroom at a more complex level. They were more adaptive in their teaching style, more flexible and tolerant. Also these teachers were more responsive to individual differences and employed a variety of teaching models, such as lectures, small group discussions, inquiry, role-playing. They were less directive and authoritative. These teachers were also more empathic; they could more accurately "read" and respond to the emotions of their students. Overall, they provided a wide and varied learning environment for their students. They were rated as effective teachers.

The work of Hunt and his associates has also demonstrated that individuals at more concrete levels of conceptual development function best in more structured environments while those at more abstract levels can function effectively in either high or low structured environments. Obviously all learners will function in different environments, but the degree of effectiveness and satisfaction will differ. Therefore, a staff development program must design appropriate, efficacious learning environments. For example, a loosely structured staff development activity will not accommodate the needs of the more concrete conceptual-level participants, so they will not function as effectively as they would in a more highly structured environment. Another pertinent example is found in the administrative characteristics of high conceptual-level educators. Silver (1975) reported that administrators at high conceptual levels were more effective in democratic leadership styles than lower conceptual-level administrators. In addition, the high conceptual level administrators were both more person-oriented and professionally-oriented while including democratic decision-making processes in their leadership.

While individuals differ in conceptual development and these differences require differentiated learning environments for optimal development it must be noted that adult growth is continuous. The developmental level of an individual is *not* to be seen as a permanent classification, but rather as a *current preferred mode* of functioning (Hunt, 1974). This perspective must be underscored to fully appreciate the developmental nature of adult growth.

Cognitive Development

Two lines of research specifically in the area of cognitive development have suggested that adults differ in their developmental status. First, there is increasing data which indicate that a large proportion of adults have not completed the transition between concrete (characterized by logical operations) and formal operational thought (characterized by propositional thinking) as evidenced on Piagetian tasks (Tomlinson-Keasy, 1972; Kuhn, Langer, Kohlberg, and Haan, 1971; Neimark, 1975). Obvious differences exist among individuals in (1) their capacity to imagine alternative combinations of variables or conditions, formulate hypotheses, systematically test these hypotheses, and (2) the awareness of one's own processes of reasoning and the ability to be critical of these processes.

Second, there is additional research that suggests a developmental sequence in thinking processes beyond Piaget's formal operations. The existence of a stage beyond formal operations was suggested on theoretical grounds by some authors (Riegel, 1973). More recently Kitchener (1977) has found evidence for the development of what she calls Reflective Judgment. This thinking process appears to build upon formal operations and go beyond it to allow individuals to make intelligent judgments in situations where information is incomplete.

In a group of 60 individuals, 20 high school juniors, 20 college juniors, and 20 advanced liberal arts graduate students, Kitchener found that there was a regular increase with *age* in scores on her measure of Reflective Judgment. In the graduate student population (an age group which approximates the age of many of those engaged in staff development) she found a range of Reflective Judgment scores from 2 to 7 on a 7-point scale. Thus, even in an adult population which one might assume would all have high scores on a measure of Reflective Judgment, wide variance was found.

Interpersonal Development

Research related to interpersonal development has provided results analogous to the results in cognitive development. Loevinger's (1976) theory of Ego Development represents a succession of turning points, or milestone sequences, that include aspects of thought, character development, interpersonal relations, and self-understanding. Research (Bernier, 1976; Oja, 1977) indicates that teachers normatively score at the conscientious/conformist and conscientious stages (about midpoint on the Loevinger scale) rather than at more advanced stages of ego development which are associated with increased flexibility, differentiation of feelings, respect for individuality, and tolerance for conflict and ambiguity.

Conceptual Systems Theory, as developed by Harvey, Hunt, and Schroder (1961), views adult development as progressing through four identifiable levels. At Level I the individual is undifferentiating and tied to social norms while processing information in a relative, simplistic manner. The highest level (Level IV) characterizes individuals as autonomous and self-reliant. Harvey and others (1966) reported that of 1400 college undergraduate and graduate students tested, approximately 1000 were classifiable as being at predominantly one of these four stages (as opposed to having evidence of more than one stage in their responses). The percentages of the 1000 classifiable individuals at the various levels were as follows: Level I—42%; Level II—21%; Level III—28%; Level IV—9%. Santmire (1979) collected data on populations including junior high school students, college sophomores, college juniors, graduate students, and parents, and also reported discernible differences in these populations according to conceptual level.

Differences among educators on both the interpersonal and cognitive dimensions are discernible. It is in the best interests of all individuals involved that these developmental differences be taken into account when designing a staff development program.

Developmental Differences and Behavior

There is some research on how differences in cognitive and interpersonal development among teachers affects how they do in inservice or staff development programs. Hunt and Joyce (1967), for example, found that high conceptual level teachers were more reflective in their teaching styles and more helpful to students in evaluating information and generating hypotheses than low conceptual level teachers. Studies by Tomlinson and Hunt (1971) and Gordon (1976) reported that low conceptual level preservice teachers preferred to teach using a rule/example order (general principles or rules stated first and then examples given), whereas high conceptual level teachers preferred to teach using an example/rule order (first providing an example and then determining a rule or principle to govern the example).

Research also strongly suggests that high conceptual level individuals can form at least two concepts about the same elements of information, that is, they are able to identify a course of action and alternatives to that action (Schroder, Driver, and Streufert, 1967; Schroder, 1971). They are also more stress tolerant (Suedfeld, 1974), better able to look at a problem from multiple viewpoints (Wolfe, 1963), create more diverse learning settings for their students (Hunt and Joyce, 1967), and function best with discovery types of learning (McLachlan and Hunt, 1973).

Both Salyachvin (1972) and Bents (1978) reported that when two different kinds of information were presented to low conceptual level students (teachers in this case) they were most affected by what they experienced first. In sum, it can be stated that less mature, less complex teachers process experience differently and may not do well in certain inservice contexts.

Development Change

To this point, we have been discussing adult development. Development has been defined here in a generic manner in terms of the cognitive complexity and information processing abilities of the individual. Developmental change affects the "structural constitution" of the individual's thinking, his/her overt pattern or way of thinking. As development progresses to higher levels of complexity, it increases the flexibility of the individual and allows the individual to react to ever-increasing stimuli.

In an educative sense, behavior can be stated in the context of desired change or objectives. Hunt (1971) described two kinds of objectives. The first are developmental (genotypic) objectives which emphasize changes in the underlying processes of structural organization of the person. Educational objectives of this type seek to alter the developmental growth of the person. On the other hand, contemporaneous (phenotypic) objectives are concerned with producing immediate, observable changes. They address specific behavioral change.

Since developmental levels of an individual are not permanent but rather are a current preferred mode of functioning, a program designer should take into account the current status of the individual and also create programs which will stimulate growth to other levels. While there is no model to stimulate developmental growth, guidelines for the development of such a model are provided by Sprinthall and Sprinthall (1980). The following aspects of their staff development efforts proved effective in promoting developmental growth:

1. Significant *role-taking experiences* such as cross-role teaching and internships should be encouraged. Each teacher should be expected to perform new, more complex interpersonal tasks than previously performed. These role-taking experiences should be experience-based, that is, they must be grounded in real, everyday activities. The experiences must be active and direct as opposed to vicarious and indirect. For example, a teacher placed in a "consulting teacher" role (where the teacher does not engage in direct instruction of pupils but rather engages in consulting functions with other teachers) would certainly be expected to perform

more complex interpersonal tasks than previously performed. This role is active and directly tied to the realities of day-to-day experience.

2. Continuing the example, assuming appropriate structure is provided to the consulting teacher role, the qualitative aspects of experience-based role-taking are taken into account. Role-taking can be either educative or miseducative contingent upon the "match" of the teacher's developmental level and the structure of the educational environment or in this example, the role of the consulting teacher. Simply stated, developmentally mature individuals will function well in either high or low structured environments. Developmentally immature individuals will function best in high structured environments. L. Sprinthall (1978) reported that when developmentally immature school supervisors were mismatched with developmentally mature student teachers, the supervisor's effectiveness ratings of these students were low. However, a more objective rating indicated a high degree of effectiveness by the mature student teachers.

3. Careful and continuous guided *reflection* is needed. When role-taking experiences (consulting teacher role, for example) are undertaken, the individual needs to examine that experience from a variety of views. This reflection can be guided by providing theoretical foundations of adult development as a baseline for questions and reactions to the role-taking experience. An understanding of adult growth and development is useful to the consulting teacher to inform her/him of the changes than can be expected when engaging in role-taking experiences. In addition, the exploration of the major tenets of developmental theory will allow the consulting teacher to reflect on her/his activity relative to the pattern of changes that all adults experience. Framed questions such as "What does this mean for me?" and "What does this mean for others?" focus and stimulate this reflection.

4. *Balance* between real experience and discussion/reflection needs to be established. Appropriate time should be provided for discussions of various experiences. Concurrently, time needs to be provided for reflection. The inservice organizer should provide a knowledge base concerning adult growth and development to serve both discussion and reflection. A guided integration is necessary to structure questions and activities. Time should be allowed for specific responsibilities. A theoretical base should be evident. And, finally, follow-up sessions should be planned.

5. The programs need to be *continuous*. Yarger, Howey, and Joyce (1980) clearly document the ineffectiveness of brief, episodic, weekend-type activities. Continuity can be provided by designing activities that extend over long periods of time. Grouping or clustering teachers provides another type of continuity both for support of the individual and for

continuous supervision. It is important to integrate inservice activities into larger program goals and objectives. In the aforementioned example of the consulting teacher, a year or even two to three years would provide the necessary continuity. To ensure lasting impact the specific activities of the consulting teacher should be integrated into larger organizational goals and objectives.

6. Both *personal support* and *challenge* should be provided. The cognitive dissonance which accompanies developmental change usually provides the necessary challenge but the program design must include appropriate psychological support. The support can come in many forms including the creation of peer support groups and a heightened awareness that adult developmental change can and does happen with everyone.

The above general guidelines are rooted in the assumptions of learning by doing and reflecting—the notion that humans grow and develop through programs that combine action and reflection. Again, these program elements are intended to stimulate *developmental* growth. It was suggested in number two above that an "appropriate" educational environment be provided for a given developmental level. We turn our attention now toward a specific example of how developmental stage differences call for different staff development approaches.

Stage Differences and Staff Development

Tailoring staff development programs to individual developmental needs and specific learning styles has the potential for making teachers more effective. In addition, the teacher is subject to change as further development occurs. *"The possibility that development continues in the adult years means that staff development programs may be playing a role, not only in teaching new content and new skills, but also in the development of the individual in more fundamental ways as well"* (Santmire, 1979).

The example used here will be that of Hunt (1966, 1971) and Hunt and Sullivan (1974) who propose a matching model to facilitate adult learning and enhance developmental growth. They suggest that each stage in conceptual development has its own characteristics that govern how information processing occurs. Each stage, they argue, has basic requisites which must be accomplished prior to transition to the next stage (for example, before an individual moves to Stage II, he/she must be able to differentiate between self and social norms). They propose that if training environments are constructed to match or be consistent with the current stage characteristics of the individual and also recognize and facilitate the requisites of that stage, they will be maximally effective in both learning and developmental senses. In brief, this matching principle states that less developmentally mature individuals profit most from highly structured environments, and more developmentally mature individuals can profit from either high or low structured environments.

To illustrate how matching might occur, we will look at development in terms of Conceptual Systems Theory (Harvey, Hunt, and Schroder, 1961). Conceptual Systems Theory is chosen as an example because this concept of development includes dimensions of both interpersonal maturity and information processing. The developmental sequence of the theory will be described in terms of the characteristics of each stage or conceptual level and the conceptual work required for progression from one level to the next. Use of this concept in the design of staff development programs will be illustrated for learners at various stages of development.

The Developmental Sequence of Conceptual Systems Theory

There are excellent descriptions of the theoretical properties of these levels in the developmental sequence described in the literature on Conceptual Systems Theory. However, to be practical for staff development planners, this sequence needs to be stated in terms of the kinds of orientations found in day-to-day experience. Therefore, the following overview translates the more theoretical treatments into the experience of teachers. The theory identifies a sequence of four stages called Conceptual Levels with three Transitional Levels between them. (This portion of the chapter draws heavily from the work of Santmire [1979]. Her articulation of conceptual levels and the notions regarding staff development are liberally used here.)

Level I. During early adolescence, most individuals have internalized the general norms and social conventions which apply to individuals within the culture or group. Everyone, including oneself, is regarded as similar with respect to these norms. Authority is respected as the source of new ideas and the determiner of right and wrong. The requisite conceptualization at this level is being able to articulate and define these norms and how they apply in one's everyday life.

Transition to Level II. At this point, the application of the norms defined at Level I makes it apparent to the individual that there are situations in which these norms appear to conflict or appear not to apply at all. This generally occurs in situations where individuals do something regarded as being appropriate from one point of view, but as inappropriate from another. The individual then questions the norms in terms of their applicability in all situations and in terms of the purpose they serve. This questioning then leads to a recognition that one often differs from the general standard in terms of ideas of what is appropriate and why. Therefore, the Transition to Level II is a period in which generalized norms and standards are questioned. The conceptual effort at this transition level is in the articulation of the ways in which one differs from various norms.

Level II. The questioning process initiated during the transition continues. Individuals begin to realize that they are not different from *all* norms and this leads to an attempt to put together a coherent idea of the self in relation to the general norms. This organization of one's own norms and standards relative to cultural norms and standards obviously requires the articulation of one's own ideas and their comparison with cultural expectations. This is the primary conceptualization that occurs at this level. The final articulation of Level II self constitutes the formation of what is referred to by these theorists as an identity.

Transition to Level III. At this level, the definition of the self as an individual is *not* generalized to others as individuals. This leads to a greater awareness of how individuals differ in several ways. Thus the primary conceptual task at this transitional level is to articulate how others differ from the self.

Level III. Increased understanding of how each individual is unique then leads, in Level III, to an understanding of where general norms or standards are inapplicable. Individuals at this level more clearly articulate how others are unique in their own right.

Transition to Level IV. Generally, Level III individuals want to coordinate their efforts with others. They increasingly realize that it is necessary to relinquish some of their individual standards for the common good. The primary conceptual task at this transitional stage is the articulation of ways in which individuals can be coordinated to meet common goals. It results in an orientation toward developing interactions which maintain the integrity of the individuals involved while obtaining desired ends. Each group evolves its own ways of interacting which vary from task to task.

Staff Development for Learners at Different Levels

A more complete understanding of this specific developmental sequence can allow one to identify characteristics of individuals at any given level or transition. In turn one can plan specific inservice environments to accommodate individuals at different stages and promote further development as well. This process is illustrated below.

Recall again that the developmental status of an individual will determine specific characteristics of everyday behavior. This will be especially observable in terms of both cognitive functioning and interpersonal orientation. The above theoretical characteristics are translated here into behaviors of teachers as learners. Inservice programs are then "matched" to these developmental characteristics. Since the majority of adult learners (including teachers) are currently assessed at Level I and Transition to Level II (Santmire, 1979), the following discussion will focus on staff development oriented to these levels.

Level I Learners and Staff Development. Level I learners are, first of all, oriented toward the practical. They are concerned with determining what to do in particular situations. Because they use their own categories (determined primarily by external events or people and isolated one from another) to organize the world, these learners find it hard to employ broad philosophical systems or principles in deciding what to do. They do not see much need for new knowledge unless they perceive that what they are doing is not working. Consequently, they often have difficulty identifying areas in which they would like *additional* training.

Level I learners are often threatened by change because of their right-wrong orientation. When innovations are presented, they may infer that the new direction must be "correct" and that what they have been doing is "incorrect." This can create a somewhat defensive attitude, especially if they perceive that what they have been doing has been working. This belief that they know what works because of their experience often makes them skeptical of new ideas. They can get caught in the bind of believing that experts or "authorities" really can't be challenged and yet that they, themselves, are also right. Furthermore, they are unable to resolve this conflict.

In learning situations, Level I learners tend to want to have what they are learning presented by, or sanctioned by, an authority. This is one assurance that what they are doing is correct. They tend, however, to be somewhat disdainful of authorities who cannot translate generalized knowledge into specific terms or procedures which are related to particular classroom settings. This is compounded by the tendency of Level I individuals to view things almost exclusively in terms of their own specific situations. If they do not see the situation as consistent with their prior experience they will think that it is not relevant to them.

Staff development activities for Level I learners need to take into consideration their practical situation and specific orientation. It is critical that these learners be able to see the need for particular inservice programs in terms of their own classroom needs. Specific information about their own teaching or classroom situation may well be needed to support any new directions. The emphasis initially should be on what to do, how to do it, and the circumstances under which it should be done.

Further, program development activities for Level I learners need to be clearly organized. Expectations of learners need to be stated explicitly in such areas as procedures, dates, outcomes, and evaluations. Topics and subtopics should be presented in hierarchical organization with categories clearly defined. Outlines, sample materials, and other support materials should be organized consistent with any oral presentation to help these learners focus on what is important. Examples of how principles apply in specific situations need to be included.

Instructional methods which include the use of materials or lessons in real-life classroom settings will have a maximum potential. However, Level I learners can also learn effectively from lecture-discussion, particularly when delivered by an acknowledged authority. Again these lectures need to be related to specific situations. Discussion techniques which are oriented around general principles and multi-sided issues and which arrive at consensus tend to be less effective. Discussions by Level I learners tend to center on examples or particular applications.

The requisite developmental work of Level I is the articulation of norms or standards. Identified norms provide the rationale for much of what these teachers do. Caution must be exercised when inservice participation encourages learning too many "options" without opportunity to consolidate them with earlier experiences. For example, exposure to three variant approaches to teaching reading over four or five years' time can confuse Level I learners as much as help them.

A basic concern is for follow-up in terms of classroom application. These types of learners are rarely secure in new ventures especially at first, and Level I learners are particularly prone to abandoning activities which do not work immediately for them. They need support to determine what they might be doing incorrectly and to help them modify their teaching. When Level I learners are given opportunities and support for consolidating new learnings and reflecting on new behaviors they can often articulate questions which lead to the Transition to Level II.

Transition to Level II Learners and Staff Development. Learners who are in Transition to Level II have begun increasingly to realize that there is more than one procedure to accomplish the same end. This realization leads to an emphasis on understanding the underlying reasons for doing things any given way. Therefore, a generalized questioning attitude is evident. Interpersonally, these learners are finding out how they differ from what they perceive the normative point of view to be. Consequently, they begin more to question authority with a concomitant emphasis on expressing their own point of view.

They tend to resist mandatory staff development programs and activities presented in the manner desired by Level I learners. They tend to focus more on questions. They tend to be more interested in principles and issues and often want to develop their own applications or adaptation of these principles.

Learners in Transition to Level II, however, have not as yet clarified their own point of view. This means that while they will often be critical of the way things are conducted, they will often be unable to develop alternative perspectives on their own. Paradoxically, while these learners express a strong desire to do things on their own, they will need help in defining what they want to do and how to do it. They also like to be supported by an authority as they challenge other authority. Thus, more subtle and indirect forms of support are needed. Public confrontation must be avoided.

As learners begin to make the transition to Level II, the certainty of a right way to do certain things is lost and a period of insecurity occurs. Because it is necessary at this level that one define one's position in relation to existing norms, individuals will need much support in raising questions and assistance in clarifying their own thinking.

Inservice activities for learners in the Transition to Level II must allow opportunities for alternatives both in choice of content and how content is to be pursued. Content can be organized around problems or issues with the development of specific applications as a by-product rather than a central focus.

How the content is organized is less important than with Level I learners since learners in the Transition to Level II often want to organize content in their own way and have a say in designing the inservice experience. Discussion of a problem or issue, followed by a presentation of the various points of view relative to the issue, concluded by a rationale for why the various points of view are held is an effective procedure. Follow-up should allow individuals to express their own point of view and develop applications for their specific classroom but with support from "authorities."

A most important consideration in staff development for learners in the Transition to Level II is the *relation* between the learners and instruction. Lecture is but tolerated as a mode of information transmission and it is best engaged in when the learner wants specific information.

Lecture-discussion in which learners have the opportunity to question and express their own point of view and have it accepted is more palatable. Group discussion techniques are preferred especially when participants are given opportunity to express and elaborate their own points of view.

The opportunity to work individually in applying newly learned principles to classroom activities is a very important part of staff development for learners in the Transition to Level II. However, because learners at this stage will often not be able to reach a group consensus, they need to engage in individually-oriented activities as well as group formats. This may be facilitated by providing assistance to these individuals in implementing their own ideas in their own classrooms.

While learners in Transition to Level II are secure in the knowledge that they will be allowed to question and that they will be supported in their attempts to explore, they will begin to think about what they themselves believe to be important rather than simply questioning for the sake of questioning. This eventually will produce the more self-directed individuals of Level II.

In summary, we have tried to illustrate the differences in the characteristics of optimum staff development for teachers at two lower but distinctly different stages of development. Different considerations for teachers at other developmental levels exist as well. Individuals at Level III, for example, would be expected to organize more of their own instruction and need increasingly individualized staff development. Democratic decision-making procedures are particularly applicable at this level. By involving the teachers in the planning processes as well as the delivery of inservice they are able to express their own uniqueness. Concurrently, as the teachers are democratically involved in the staff development procedures they are better able to appreciate and understand general norms and standards.

As adult learners move from Level III to higher levels they would be expected to engage in more team types of arrangements and focus upon more complex and cross-cutting concerns. The requisite articulation of individual uniqueness attained in Level III forms the basis for collaborative efforts with others. Staff development concerns at Level IV take the form of supporting the numerous staff renewal suggestions generated by these individuals. Support and opportunity to exercise options would characterize programs for individuals of high conceptual level maturity.

Remember these are only examples of some generalizable differences about one dimension of adult development. The point we wish to make is that developmental differences exist in adult learners and are in fact manifested in characteristics which affect what they learn in staff developmental programs.

Developmental Age Differences

Like the stage theorists reviewed earlier, age theorists also provide us with insights into inservice programming. Age theorists take chronological age as the major variable in the search for characteristics associated with particular periods in the lives of adults. Corrigan, Haberman, and Howey (1979) note:

> Were we to take one persistent problem commonly addressed in programs of inservice education, such as discipline, we are confident we could find significant differences in how this is viewed on the basis of sex and age of teachers. There may well be similar differences with respect to communication, teacher expectation, grading, parental relations, and other common topics focused upon inservice (p. 26).

Indeed, age-related factors should be considered when planning inservice programs. For example, age-linked behavior popularized by Sheehy (1976) in her book *Passages* might be considered. The tentative synthesis offered by Sheehy identifies six age related categories: (1.) 16-22 Pulling Up Roots; (2.) 22-29 Provisional Adulthood; (3.) 29-32 Age Thirty Transition; (4.) 32-39 Rooting; (5.) 39-43 Mid-Life Transition; and (6.) 43-50 Restabilization and Flowering. An inservice activity designed to teach cooperative goal structures would generally be met with different response from individuals in the 32-39 "Rooting" category than those individuals in the 39-43 "Mid-Life Transition."

Those in the 32-39 age category would probably view this activity as an opportunity to widen and stabilize their base of support. The activities accompanying cooperative goal structures could allow for deepened collaborative commitments and a clearer vision of working toward longer-term goals. On the other hand, these cooperative activities might accentuate the personal discomfort experienced by the 39-43 individual in mid-life transition. As this individual faces the gap between youthful dreams and their actual fulfillment, a more personalized, self-searching activity may well be more appropriate. Regardless of the activity provided, however, differences related to age should not be ignored. Increasingly information gained from teachers with respect to their staff development "needs" should be examined in terms of age-related patterns and concerns.

Yarger and Mertens (1979) have identified various teaching career stages which can be viewed as "professional age" variables. They posit six different career stages of teachers and outline inservice programming which is appropriate to the needs of each professional stage. The first two stages are concerned with the pre-education student and the education student, respectively. Although these stages are primarily dealt with in preservice programs it is important for inservice program planners to be cognizant of the concerns, content, foundations, methods, and clinical programming occurring at these stages. It is important that these early stages be considered a part of the continuum of professional development. The inservice program can either reflect this continuous progression by *building* on the early experiences of teachers or, as is so often the situation, they can be viewed as two sets of unrelated experiences and actually work counter to one another.

The initial or beginning teacher is moving from the relative security of a training program to the complex demands of the teaching profession and needs to be supported in that transition. Concerns about classroom discipline, further developing pedagogical skills, and receiving specific, immediate feedback highlight this stage. This developing teacher, according to Yarger and Mertens, has successfully completed the first year but is still a novice professional. Beginning teacher concerns still exist, but concern about content, "gaps" in previous training, and realizing that things do change emerge as well.

The practicing teacher (3-8 years of experience) is more stable. Teachers at this stage are generally tenured, have advanced certification or degrees, and have demonstrated their ability to function in the classroom. Content expertise is a high priority for this group as well as preparation for a new professional role (team leader, department chairperson, "special" areas teacher, administrator).

The final stage is the experienced teacher. Motivation for the experienced teacher to become involved in inservice activities often varies from that of their less experienced colleagues. It is particularly important to engage these experienced teachers in well-designed professional assessment activities. This will not only encourage them to reflect upon what they are doing personally, but also creates an avenue for them to share their expertise.

Staff development programs must be responsive not only in the context of a curriculum issue or teaching approach but also in terms of the personal/professional development of the teacher. As one works with teachers, it becomes obvious that teachers have concerns about changes or innovations. We now turn our attention to a framework which enables the systematic inclusion of teachers' concerns in staff development.

Concerns-Based Development

As we know, teachers' concerns are due not only to individual differences but to individual differences as they *interact* with specific innovations or changes called for in staff development efforts. Thus, information regarding teachers' concerns about a specific innovation or change are particularly useful in planning inservice. The following model assists

---

Figure 1. Stages of Concern About the Innovation*

Stage 6 REFOCUSING: The focus is on exploration of more universal benefits from the innovation, including the possibility of major changes or replacement with a more powerful alternative. Individual has definite ideas about alternatives to the proposed or existing form of the innovation.

Stage 5 COLLABORATION: The focus is on coordination and cooperation with others regarding use of the innovation.

Stage 4 CONSEQUENCE: Attention focuses on impact of the innovation on students in his/her immediate sphere of influence. The focus is on relevance of the innovation for students, evaluation of student outcomes, including performance and competencies, and changes needed to increase student outcomes.

Stage 3 MANAGEMENT: Attention is focused on the processes and tasks of using the innovation, and the best use of information and resources. Issues related to efficiency, organizing, managing, scheduling, and time demands are utmost.

Stage 2 PERSONAL: Individual is uncertain about the demands of the innovation, his/her adequacy to meet those demands, and his/her role with the innovation. This includes analysis of his/her role in relation to the reward structure of the organization, decision-making and consideration, or potential conflicts with existing structures or personal commitment. Financial or status implications of the program for self and colleagues may also be reflected.

Stage 1 INFORMATIONAL: A general awareness of the innovation and interest in learning more about it is indicated. The person seems to be unworried about himself/herself in relation to the innovation. She/he is interested in substantive aspects of the innovation in a selfless manner such as general characteristics, effects, and requirements for use.

Stage 0 AWARENESS: Little concern about or involvement with the innovation is indicated.

---

* Original concept from G. E. Hall, R. C. Wallace, Jr., and W. A. Dossett, *A Developmental Conceptualization of the Adoption Process Within Educational Institutions.* (Austin: Research and Development Center for Teacher Education, The University of Texas, 1973).

in understanding concerns that teachers might have about change in general or a specific innovation.

The concept of Stages of Concern is based upon work by Frances Fuller (1969) in studying the concerns of undergraduates as they moved through phases of preservice teacher programs. Fuller found that the concerns of undergraduate education majors progressed through several levels. Their initial concerns were "unrelated" to the profession of teaching altogether, and then shifted to a "self" focus as their student teaching experience began. As the student teaching experience continued, Fuller found that undergraduates began to have more "task" concerns, focusing on the task of teaching and the logistics related to it. Ultimately, as students moved beyond task concerns, Fuller found that they began to have "impact" concerns—concerns about the consequences of their teaching and on issues related to the improvement of their teaching performance.

Hall and others (1973) expanded and generalized the concept of concerns to include seven *Stages of Concern About the Innovation*. These stages follow a similar progression from unrelated to self, task, and impact concerns. Just as the development of adults progresses through various stages, concern also progresses through various stages.

The concept of concerns focuses upon the mental gyrations, perceptions, and feelings that a teacher or administrator has in relation to a particular innovation. While these are not always well thought out or sharply focused, mental energy tends to be focused as it relates to a specific innovation.

The full definition of the *Stages of Concern About the Innovation* are described in Figure 1. Note that "Stage 2–Personal" closely approximates the Fuller concept of self-concerns while "Stage 3–Management" closely approximates what Fuller referred to as task concerns. Impact concerns are divided according to "Stage 4–Consequence," "Stage 5–Collaboration," and "Stage 6–Refocusing."

These Stages of Concern can provide a framework and diagnostic tool for determining individual teacher responses to a change introduced through an inservice activity. Just as conceptual maturity indicates the "structures" of people's thinking, the Stages of Concern provide information making it possible to predict in general what will happen to individuals as they approach and go through a change. The Concerns-Based Adoption Model (CBAM) (Hall, Wallace, and Dossett, 1973) was developed to examine the interaction between individuals and larger change efforts such as an extensive inservice project.

The Concerns-Based Adoption Model has direct implications for staff development. The model and the research related to it are based on assumptions that: (a) staff development for teachers and administrators must begin with the premise of individual differences, and (b) staff development experiences must be thought through programmatically as a *process* rather than dealt with as isolated occurrences or singular events.

As the name suggests, the Concerns-Based Adoption Model focuses upon *change*. The term innovation is used to represent the new process, product, or procedure that is being implemented. Invariably in major change efforts, a staff development program is designed to assist teachers and administrators in making the desired transition. Although teachers may not always see themselves as involved in "change," training or staff development experiences generally have as a goal, some sort of change or improvement in behavior, performance, or outcome.

Additional assumptions which underlie the Concerns-Based Adoption Model are also relevant to staff development:

A. *The change (innovation) is appropriate.* Not all innovations are positive; an innovation that might be positive in one context may have a negative consequence in another context. Underlying the CBAM is the assumption that in a particular context the innovation that is being introduced is one that is judged to be positive and have potential for positive outcomes with the users and their clients.

B. *Change is a process, not an event.* Often, decision makers and even adult learners assume that change is an event rather than a process. From the CBAM point of view, it is not possible to bring about change instantaneously through passing a law, sending a memo, holding a two-day workshop, or making an announcement in a fall faculty meeting. Rather, change is a process that has to unfold; a period of time is involved.

C. *Change is a personal experience.* There is a personal side to change; feelings, perceptions, frustrations are a natural part of change for each person involved. It is neither logical nor possible to deny the existence of this personal dimension to change and rather than deny it, we should attend to it.

D. *The individual has to be a focal point.* Individuals are members of an organization, yet, they remain individuals. In order to understand and facilitate the change process and to design relevant staff development activities, what is happening to the individual *specifically* and *collectively* must be taken into account. (The critical organizational variables which provide the ecological perspective are discussed in Chapter 3. The focus here is on the individual and how he/she experiences the change process.)

E. *Change entails growth.* Not only is change a process as it is experienced by the individual within an organization but there are identifiable steps in terms of growth that an individual can move through. Developmental growth in feelings about change are defined in the concept of Stages of Concern About the Innovation (Hall, 1979) .

These assumptions again provide guidelines that are helpful in the design of a staff development program. It is not possible to design a program based on these assumptions without attending to individuals. Further, it is proposed that the staff development program should take into account an individual's Stage of Concern in deciding what staff development might be most appropriate. This does not rule out providing for individuals in various types of groups, but it does suggest that the membership of those groups should be carefully considered in the design of staff development interventions.

Stages of Concern About the Innovation can be assessed several ways. One procedure entails first-hand contact with a teacher in a variety of settings. Informal conversations yield much information regarding an individual's stage of concern. Another method that can be employed is the use of an open-ended questionnaire (Newlove and Hall, 1976) . In this procedure respondents are asked to describe their concerns on a blank piece of paper that has stated at the top:

When you think about   (change or innovation)   , what are you concerned about? (Do not say what you think others are concerned about, but only what concerns you.) Please write in complete sentences, and please be frank.

This written statement can readily be coded according to the seven levels of concern, shown in Figure 1, to determine which Stages of Concern are most intense for different individuals.

Yet another systematic procedure for assessing Stages of Concern is the Stages of Concern Questionnaire (Hall, George, and Rutherford, 1977) . This questionnaire makes it possible to obtain psychometrically rigorous data which can be used to construct "concerns profiles" that not only identify the most intense Stage of Concern but that also provide an indication of the relative intensity of other Stages of Concern. Again, inservice or staff development can be planned to accommodate individuals on the basis of this data. A person will have an array of concerns with some more intense than others; staff development experiences should be planned to address the areas of highest concern. Depending upon the staff development provided the intensity of the Stages of Concern may shift and new experiences can be planned.

The Concerns-Based Adoption Model presents another development dimension—one that focuses upon the interaction of *individuals* with major changes over time. From a concerns-based perspective, individuals have to be the focus for the design and delivery of staff development activities. The concept of Stages of Concern about the Innovation can also be used as a diagnostic tool and guide for the staff development program. The staff development program would be a continuing process in this scheme and would shift in its design, type of intervention, and style of delivery. Stages of Concern offers a constructive way to think about the concept of development in staff development.

Adult Learning

This chapter has, as its primary concern, the concept of adult development as it relates to staff development. However, there are some generally accepted principles for facilitating adult learning, regardless of one's stage of development, that are worth reviewing here. The following assumptions have broad-based endorsement and some empirical support. According to Knowles (1978), these principles constitute "the foundation stones of modern adult learning theory":

1. Adults are motivated to learn as they experience needs and interests that learning will satisfy; therefore, these needs and interests are appropriate starting points for organizing adult learning activities.

2. Adult orientation to learning is life-centered; therefore, the appropriate units for organizing adult learning are life situations, not subjects.

3. Experience is the richest resource for adult learning; therefore, the core methodology of adult education is the analysis of experience.

4. Adults have a deep need to be self-directing; therefore, the role of the teacher is to engage in a process of mutual inquiry rather than to transmit knowledge to them and then evaluate their conformity to it.

5. Individual differences among people increase with age; therefore, adult education must make optimal provision for differences in style, time, place, and pace of learning (p. 31).

We would qualify some of these statements since we are convinced that while adults are often self-directing, engage in mutual inquiry, and, noting that teachers are inclined toward the pragmatic, there are qualitative differences. Certainly, teachers vary in the degree of self-directedness, ability and desire to work collaboratively, and competence to deal with conceptual problems and universal principles as well as practical concerns. Often these differences are related to developmental stages.

Klopf (1979) elaborates on these fundamental notions. He indicates that the clarity of role expectations, awareness of self, and opportunity to practice new skills are of utmost importance to adults in general and teachers in particular. Clarity of role expectations refers to a teacher's awareness and knowledge of his/her own role and function within the total school environment. "Whether or not the expectations for levels of performance are agreed to by the staff or are derived from the belief system of the principal, they need to be stated. Vague statements about good teaching or improving learning environments are not adequate to enable adults to learn. There needs to be a simple system which makes sense to what one is expected to learn and do" (p. 2).

Awareness of self, according to Klopf, is to "understand various role enactments." Such understanding is necessary in order to grow professionally. Therefore, adult learning takes into account the *professional performance* of teachers and *how this performance is determined* by such factors as personal goals, strengths, needs, and beliefs.

The opportunity to practice new skills is also very important for adults. In addition, Klopf notes that school personnel need supportive feedback on their performance in the new situation. They often need a collaborative atmosphere in which they can practice new approaches and analyze their effectiveness.

The uniqueness of teachers as learners must also be considered. For example, teachers are adults who spend the majority of their work day in a relatively small space with relatively large groups of young people. Parallels with other roles are hard to find. They often have minimal opportunities to interact with peers and few chances to assume different roles. The status of teachers is often suspect. Expectations for them are not only considerable but often contradictory. Teachers are often viewed as a "conduit" in staff development: they are to learn to help others learn; their personal sense of development is rarely considered.

In addition, there are other situational pressures within the school setting which affect the teacher and which should be considered in planning staff development. These are discussed in Chapter 3 on Organization Development. We underscore *teacher* as adult learner here to remind the reader that taking into account the developmental differences and learning styles of adults is not sufficient for effective inservice programs. We would also like to reinforce the basic notion on learning stated by Kurt Lewin (1935); that is, learning is a function of the *interaction* of the person and the environment. In this chapter we address aspects of one of these variables—the adult person. It is imperative that the other contextual variables as well as the *interaction* among them and the teacher be more systematically considered in planning and providing staff development. Reading this book in its entirety will help all of us reflect upon the relationships and interactions which should be considered in program staff development plans, activities, and evaluations.

REFERENCES

Bents, R. H. "A Study of the Effects of Environmental Structure on Students of Differing Conceptual Levels." Ph.D. dissertation, University of Minnesota, 1978. *Dissertation Abstracts International*, 1978, ED780286.

Bernier, J. "A Psychological Education Intervention for Teacher Development." Ph.D. dissertation, University of Minnesota, 1976. *Dissertation Abstracts International*, 1976, ED776932.

Chickering, A. K. "The Educational Needs of New Learners: Implications for Liberal Arts Colleges." Paper presented at the East Central Colleges Consortium Conference on the New Learners, December 1974.

Corrigan, D.; Haberman, M.; and Howey, K. *Adult Learning and Development: Implications for Inservice Teacher Education.* Paris: Center for Educational Research and Innovation Project on Inservice Education and Training for Teachers, 1979.

Flavell, J.; Botkin, P.; Fry, C.; Wright, J.; and Jervis, P. *Role-taking and Communications Skills in Children.* New York: John Wiley, 1968.

Fuller, F. F. "Concerns of Teachers: A Developmental Conceptualization." *American Educational Research Journal* 6,2 (1969) : 207-226.

Gordon, M. "Choice of Rule-Example Order Used to Teach Mathematics as a Function of Conceptual Level and Field-Dependence-Independence." Paper presented at the annual meeting of the American Educational Research Association, San Francisco, April 1976.

Hall, G. E. *Stages of Concern by Adults.* Position paper, 1979.

Hall, G. E.; George, A. A.; Rutherford, W. L. *Measuring Stages of Concern About the Innovation: A Manual for Use of the SoC Questionnaire.* Austin: Research and Development Center for Teacher Education, The University of Texas, 1977.

Hall, G. E.; Wallace, R. C.; and Dossett, W. A. *A Developmental Conceptualization of the Adoption Process Within Educational Institutions.* Austin: Research and Development Center for Teacher Education, The University of Texas, 1973.

Harvey, O. J.; Hunt, D. E.; and Schroder, H. M. *Conceptual Systems and Personality Organization.* New York: John Wiley, 1961.

Harvey, O. J.; White, B. J.; Prather, M. S.; Alter, R. D.; and Hoffmeister, J. K. "Teachers' Belief Systems and Preschool Atmospheres." *Journal of Educational Psychology* 57 (1966) : 373-381.

Hunt, D. E. "A Conceptual Systems Change Model and its Application to Education." In *Experience, Structure, and Adaptability*, pp. 277-302. Edited by O. J. Harvey. New York: Springer, 1966.

Hunt, D. E. *Matching Models in Education.* Toronto: Ontario Institute for Studies in Education, 1971.

Hunt, D. E., and Joyce, B. R. "Teacher Trainee Personality and Initial Teaching Style." *American Educational Research Journal* 4 (1967) : 253-259.

Hunt, D. E., and Sullivan, E. V. *Between Psychology and Education.* Hinsdale, Ill.: Dryden, 1974.

Inhelder, B., and Piaget, J. *The Growth of Logical Thinking from Childhood to Adolescence.* New York: Basic Books, 1958.

Kitchener, K. S. "Intellectual Development in Late Adolescents and Young Adults: Reflective Judgment and Verbal Reasoning." Ph.D. dissertation, University of Minnesota, 1977. *Dissertation Abstracts International*, 1977, ED813414.

Klopf, G. *Needs of the Adult Learner.* Position paper, 1979.

Knowles, M. *The Adult Learner: A Neglected Species.* Houston: Gulf, 1978.

Kuhn, D.; Langer, J.; Kohlberg, L.; and Haan, N. "The Development of Formal-Operational Thought: Its Relation to Moral Judgment." Unpublished mimeograph,

Cambridge, 1971.
Lewin, K. *A Dynamic Theory of Personality.* New York: McGraw-Hill, 1935.
Loevinger, J. *Ego Development.* San Francisco: Jossey-Bass, 1976.
McLachlan, J. F. C., and Hunt, D. E. "Differential Effects of Discovery Learning as a Function of Student Conceptual Level." *Canadian Journal of Behavioral Science* 5 (1973) : 152-160.
Neimark, E. D. "Intellectual Development During Adolescence." In *Review of Child Development Research,* Volume 4. Edited by F. D. Horowitz. Chicago: University of Chicago Press, 1975.
Newlove, B. W., and Hall, G. E. *A Manual for Assessing Open-Ended Statements of Concern About an Innovation.* Austin: Research and Development Center for Teacher Education, The University of Texas, 1976.
Oja, S. "A Cognitive-Structural Approach to Adult Ego, Moral and Conceptual Development Through Inservice Teacher Education." Ph.D. dissertation, University of Minnesota, 1977. *Dissertation Abstracts International,* 1977, ED7906363.
Riegel, K. F. "Dialectic Operations: The Final Period of Cognitive Development." *Human Development* 16 (1973) : 346-370.
Salyachvin, S. "Change in International Understanding as a Function of Perceived Similarity, Conceptual Level, and Primary Effect." Unpublished Ph.D. dissertation, University of Toronto, 1972.
Santmire, T. E. *Developmental Differences in Adult Learners: Implications for Staff Development.* Position paper, 1979.
Schroder, H. M. "Conceptual Complexity and Personality Organization." In *Personality Theory and Information Processing.* Edited by H. M. Schroder and P. Suedfield. New York: Ronald Press, 1971.
Schroder, H. M.; Driver, M. J.; and Streufert, S. *Human Information Processing.* New York: Holt, Rinehart and Winston, 1967.
Selman, R. L. "The Relation of Role-Taking to the Development of Moral Judgments in Children." *Child Development* 42 (1971) : 79-91.
Sheehy, G. *Passages: Predictable Crises of Adult Life.* New York: Dutton, 1976.
Silver, P. "Principals' Conceptual Ability in Relation to Situation and Behavior." *Educational Administrator Quarterly* 11,3 (1975) : 49-66.
Sprinthall, L. *Supervision: Educative or Miseducative Process?* Research Report. St. Cloud, Minn.: St. Cloud State University, 1978.
Sprinthall, N. A., and Sprinthall, L. T. "Adult Development and Leadership Training for Mainstream Education." In *Concepts to Guide the Teaching of Teachers of Teachers.* Edited by D. Corrigan and K. Howey. Reston, Va.: Council for Exceptional Children, 1980.
Suedfeld, P. "Attitude Manipulation in Restricted Environments: Conceptual Structure and Response to Propaganda." *Journal of Abnormal and Social Psychology* 68 (1974) : 242-247.
Tomlinson, P. D., and Hunt, D. E. "Differential Effect of Rule-Example Order as a Function of Learner Conceptual Level." *Canadian Journal of Behavioral Science* 3 (1971) : 237-245.
Tomlinson-Keasy, C. "Formal Operations in Females from Eleven to Fifty-four Years of Age." *Developmental Psychology* 6 (1972) : 364.
Tomlinson-Keasy, C., and Keasy, C. B. "The Mediating Role of Cognitive Development in Moral Judgment." *Child Development* 45 (1974) : 291-299.
Wolfe, R. "The Role of Conceptual Systems in Cognitive Functioning at Varying Levels of Age and Intelligence." *Journal of Personality* 31 (1963) : 108-123.
Yarger, S. J., and Mertens, S. K. "Testing the Waters of School-Based Teacher Education." In *Concepts to Guide the Teaching of Teachers of Teachers.* Edited by D. Corrigan and K. Howey. Reston, Va.: Council for Exceptional Children, 1980.
Yarger, S. J.; Howey, K. R.; Joyce, B. R. *Inservice Teacher Education.* Palo Alto, Calif.: Booksend Laboratory, 1980.

3

Staff Development and Organization Development

Albert E. Roark and Wallace E. Davis, Jr.

ORGANIZATION DEVELOPMENT is an emergent discipline that provides concepts and skills for improving the climate and problem-solving ability of organizations. Applied to education, its goal is to help members of school organizations (faculties, administrators, community members) develop communities which effectively solve problems, initiate needed changes, and provide support for their members.

Educational change can come about as a reaction to initiatives and pressures from outside the school, as a result of problems felt inside the school, and as part of a continuous process of improving the organization. Albert Roark and Wallace Davis have summarized the core of Organization Development content and how it can be used by educators to create the kind of organization that will seek ways of improving itself, initiating change, and reacting responsibility and sensitively to the community.

Hence, OD concepts and skills can be the *substance* of inservice programs. They can also facilitate the creation of staff development systems and specifically-targeted projects.

AT SOME POINT in each school year designated individuals turn their attention to developing inservice education programs. Although all of them hope to design programs that are well accepted and effective, a sizeable number of the programs are considered a waste of time by participants. What gremlin produces these failures? Are there steps the designers could take to minimize the risks? In the following paragraphs these questions are addressed by examining three hypothetical inservice situations.

• SITUATION 1. An outside consultant is asked to present a program to a nearby school district. When he asks them what they want, he is told that since he is familiar with the district he should do whatever he thinks appropriate. The program he presents is entertaining and enlightening. The evaluation, conducted immediately after the presentation, indicates that the participants judged it to be a success and that the consultant should be invited to return. However, when inservice as an

37

activity is discussed later, the overwhelming sentiment is that the district's inservice efforts are not very effective. What went wrong?

• SITUATION 2. A districtwide program for elementary teachers is designed to introduce a team teaching strategy the assistant superintendent for instruction has ordered implemented next fall. Consultants who believe in team teaching and who have successfully implemented similar programs in other school districts are brought in to conduct the inservice. The evaluation conducted at the close of the inservice indicates that most participants feel the sessions were worthwhile and they would support the implementation of the team teaching program. However, when the degree of acceptance is measured one year after implementation, it is found that acceptance is mostly verbal. In addition, even though the inservice program included strategies for winning parental support, parents continue to resist the concept of team teaching and the performance of students on standardized tests has declined. Why did such a well planned and implemented inservice program fail?

• SITUATION 3. A school district where teachers exhibit a negative attitude toward inservice polls its faculty about the type of inservice they desire. Those programs receiving the greatest support are then offered. Evaluations conducted at the end of the inservice indicate that most teachers feel that the programs provided meet their needs and should be continued. Yet, during the following year, little change in teacher effectiveness is noted. Teachers who had been successful prior to their participation continue to be successful, while those who had experienced difficulties continue to exhibit the same behavior. In addition, when inservice is discussed the following year, the general attitude of teachers continues to be negative. Why did programs designed around the desires of teachers have so little effect, and why did teacher attitude concerning inservice remain negative?

In each of these situations, the inservice designers failed to consider the setting within which their programs were offered. The setting is the organization. Organizational phenomena, rather than fate, timing, or desire, defeated each of these inservice efforts. Effective programs operate within the basic tenets and forces created by the organizational characteristics of the school. Violating these tenets can only harm program quality.

To appreciate this we must begin with a highly simplified definition of the school as an organization. It can be defined as a collection of interacting groups, each seeking some personal reward, but all motivated by some common purpose or goal. Its existence depends on the continuing belief that this purpose can be attained more effectively or efficiently by collective rather than individual action. While not perfect, this definition can serve to identify some of the organizational forces that influenced the three hypothetical inservice designs presented earlier.

In the first situation, with the entertaining consultant, there was no purpose serving as the driving force for the inservice program except that provided by the consultant. Organizations exist to fulfill goals considered worthwhile by those who support or sustain them. People are goal-oriented and goal-motivated (Hoy, 1978); when they are adrift, without purpose, plan, or destination, morale suffers. Declining morale in turn hampers effectiveness. Although the teachers enjoyed and to some degree were enlightened by the consultant, the lack of a goal-oriented purpose was apparent. Their initial favorable response to his efforts were based on their reaction to the presenter rather than to the organizational effectiveness of his program. Later, when they looked back in light of such effectiveness, they found the program lacking.

In the second situation, there was an underlying purpose for the inservice design: to implement a team teaching program. However, the purpose was supplied by a school district official who, because of his position, considered himself to be a unilateral decision maker. As such, he neglected the "collection of interacting groups" aspect of the definition of the organization. His role in the school system was not independent of those of teachers and parents; rather, all three roles were interdependent. Therefore, his success as a leader depended significantly on their willingness to follow. His first mistake was in assuming that the teachers would willingly abandon an organizational pattern that had evolved over time and that they supported. Teachers are not automatons. Their behavior is never purely mechanical. They cannot be programmed exclusively by the expectations of any administrator, regardless of his or her position. Any administrative demand that requires teachers to set aside some part of their values or needs is literally a depersonalizing demand and can result in teacher dissatisfaction and decreased effectiveness (Katz and Kahn, 1978).

The assistant superintendent's second mistake was in assuming that the school district, at the time of his proposal, was a peaceful millpond awaiting the rippling of his ideas. Rather, it was a field of competing forces for and against each educational program, each instructional process, and each organizational arrangement (Davis, 1972). The current situation is best described as a temporary balance of such forces. The administrator's decision to change from the established organizational pattern indicated to the teachers that he considered their present method of instructional organization unsatisfactory and inefficient. They felt comfortable in their organization and resented his efforts to alter something they strongly supported. Their attitude, strengthened by the organization's built-in resistance to change, defeated this district's inservice effort (Hoy, 1978).

In the third situation, the purpose was again unilateral rather than organizational but this time it was supplied by the teachers based on their needs as individuals rather than as members of a school district. In polling the teachers, the designer disregarded the central goal that must unite each school district: to prepare students for their adult roles (Hoy, 1978). In this instance, the central goal was displaced by a much narrower one. Although tempting, focusing on the individual needs of teachers disregards the organizational reality that school systems exist for those who support them. We sometimes act as if parents and communities have no choice in whether they participate in the educational process. However, this perception is hardly tenable considering the number of communities who castigate their schools by rejecting bond issues and refusing to increase tax levies. It seems even less tenable considering the increasing number of parents who choose private over public schools.

Historically, teachers have been motivated by the desire to serve. When they feel their service is unappreciated, morale declines and this in turn affects efficiency. Although the inservice program described in situation three met their personal desires, and therefore received a favorable evaluation, viewed in retrospect, its lack of goal relevance offended the teachers' sense of professionalism. This, in turn, led to their negative feelings concerning inservice in general.

The situations discussed in the preceding paragraphs illustrate instances where inservice designers failed to consider organizational realities. Such oversight suggests that today's highly organized and increasingly bureaucratic school systems need organizational development and renewal that differs from traditional inservice efforts. While such a process may sound utopian, it is currently available. It is the process of Organization Development, generally referred to as OD. Although it has been around about 20 years, its effectiveness as a strategy for the organizational renewal of school systems has not been uniformly positive. When properly used, however, a growing research base indicates that it can make a substantial impact on the problems that face today's designers of inservice programs. Its strength is that it views the organization as an interacting whole rather than as a set of independent parts. Its promise is such, that no school district should discount it before examining its possibilities.

OD Defined

Some feel that organization development, like the nongraded classroom, may be more a state of mind than a strategy for organizational renewal. There is no generally accepted definition of OD; in fact, the multitude of definitions led one writer to note "no more definitions, please" (Filmore, 1974). If one examines the various definitions available some common characteristics emerge. These are:

1. The OD strategy systematically confronts the tension that exists between individual freedom and the constraints on that freedom imposed by the demand for organizational productivity.

2. The OD strategy systematically addresses the relationship between the product sought and the process used to achieve that product.

3. The OD strategy systematically seeks commitment by involving all of those with some stake in the organization in information gathering, program solving, and decision making.

4. The OD strategy seeks to become a regular and ongoing function of the school system.

While it may be productive in the long run to omit formulating yet another definition and simply view OD efforts in the light of these characteristics, a working definition can prove helpful. Based on this assumption, the following definition developed by the Participative Option Development Project is offered:

We define OD as a participatory, data-based process for improving working relationships, programs, student learning, and school climate within a school organization. The process is facilitated through systematic goal setting, planning, human relations development, decision making, problem solving, and assessment procedures (Martin, Roark, and Tonso, 1978a, p. 4).

School systems that undertake organization development must understand that OD involves more than the name OD. It involves all of the elements listed earlier. Neglecting any of them will result in a program that may work too hard for too little, thereby limiting the potential that OD offers.

However, if all of these elements are used in a relational and balanced way, a school system can expect certain benefits, including the following:

1. OD can provide long-range effort to introduce planned improvements;

2. OD can secure the commitment of those affected by these improvements by drawing upon the talents of the total school community;

3. OD can assist a school district in defining and achieving its goals by creating conditions in which individuals and groups can collaborate to utilize their full potential;

4. OD can stimulate a cross-pollination of ideas within a school; and

5. OD can begin school improvement efforts from the ongoing activities of the school rather than "from scratch" (Martin, Roark, and Tonso, 1978a, p. 4).

Organizational Issues Addressed by OD

Organization development typically addresses several issues. The most common of these, Goal Alignment, Task and Process, Information, Functional Criteria, and Choices and Commitments, are discussed here.

Goal Alignment

As individuals we each have needs which unless fulfilled to a satisfactory degree will cause some discomfort or diminished functioning. Buildings, whether they are large metropolitan high schools or small country elementary schools, also have needs which must be satisfied if they are to be effective, "good" schools.

Organization needs, especially at the building and school district level, are often written down and published as specific goals. Students, teachers, and community members do not specify their goals as precisely. The fact that they are not precisely spelled out, however, does not mean that they do not exist. Nor, does it mean that vague and indistinct goals are not as important as the ones that are written in handbooks and brochures.

Problems occur when formal and informal goals come in conflict creating a traffic jam which can disrupt school effectiveness. OD enters with the explicit intent of reducing the size, number, and effect of traffic jams and snarls if any are found. This is accomplished by assessing needs from the individual to the community level and, where possible, aligning the goals derived from these needs.

Once goals are aligned, all goal-directed activities will at least be compatible. This may not be the case, however, if reliance on common resource pools and the use of incompatible activities to achieve similar goals create difficulty. OD works to uncover these difficulties and conceptualize them as problems to be solved for mutual benefit.

The idea in goal alignment is to develop goals that are compatible so that all goals represented from individual to school district meet community goal expectations. The process is envisioned as a collaborative one in which all relevant parties participate in developing the goals they are expected to work toward (Stewart, 1973).

Relationship of Goals to Procedures and Activities

Goals lead to procedures and activities. Organization development intends to accomplish three basic objectives relative to procedures. One is to determine if people are doing what they believe they are doing. The second objective is to determine how well what they are doing serves to accomplish their goals. The third objective is to determine how people feel about what they are doing. For example, if an attendance policy intended to reduce absenteeism calls for phone contacts with the parents or guardians on the first two absences and a parent-teacher-principal visit on the third and succeeding absences, OD would call for (1) determining how faithfully the phone calls and visits are made, (2) seeing if there is evidence that the contacts reduce absences, and (3) finding out how the staff involved feels about using the system. This information is then used to help people choose or design activities to achieve a situation where all goals are compatible and all activities are goal-directed, compatible, and personally desirable (Weisborg, 1976).

Individual rights, expectations, rewards, and constraints are frequent sources of difficulty in any organization. These issues are exacerbated in public schools because the school is part of the community on one hand and an organization with a job to do on the other. This is further complicated because society has not decided clearly what is expected of public education. Teachers have perceptions of what their rights, expectations, rewards, and constraints should be; which not only vary considerably among individuals but are changing for the profession as a whole. Organization development endeavors to help people from community members to students, teachers, and administrators articulate their positions in these areas and work out mutually satisfactory arrangements (Hess and Greenstein, 1972). Organization development is not considered to extend to litigation, arbitration, or negotiations, although it obviously influences the conduct of these activities. OD generally limits its legitimate domain to formal and informal everyday activities.

Task and Process

Any job or activity has two basic dimensions, commonly referred to as task and process. Basically, task refers to *what* is done and process refers to *how* it is done. For example, if a decision is to be made, the task would be making the decision. The process would be the way the decision is made. In this case, it is obvious that how the decision is made would strongly influence participants' emotional reactions to the decision.

Personal feelings help determine how effectively a task is accomplished. If they are positive feelings such as enthusiasm and satisfaction, they will help. Negative feelings, such as resentment and apathy, can be expected to hinder task accomplishment. The task itself can lead to emotions that influence the accomplishment of subsequent tasks. The interdependence of task and process is complicated but usually is conceptualized as the degree to which process facilitates task accomplishment.

OD analyzes the processes used to accomplish tasks with the intent of discovering to what extent process issues may be hindering the accomplishment of tasks (Weisborg, 1976). Analysis is also done to see if the process used seems to be the most appropriate process available for the task. For example, if decision making is the task, does the process lead to good decisions that people are committed to carry out? And, is the process cost effective in terms of time and money? One district (well aware of this point) faced with declining enrollment and escalating expenses needed to cut back on costs. Central office staff determined that reducing the number of periods taught would be the most feasible manner to reduce costs sufficiently. However, instead of simply saying that this would be done, the possibility was announced and building personnel were encouraged to find more desirable alternatives. In subsequent investigation supported by the central office, building personnel could not find another satisfactory way to reduce costs as much as necessary but they learned to appreciate the dilemma and supported the necessary change. The process had led to support of what started out as a very unpopular solution. OD considers the task-process "fit" one of the more important elements in efficient organizational functioning (Berman and McLaughlin, 1978).

Information

The third issue considered in OD is the degree to which an organization operates on valid information. Three elements are analyzed. One is how much total information is available and how available it is to decision makers. The second element is whether this information is sufficient for efficient operation of the organization. The third element or question is whether the information available is sufficiently valid for organizational needs. For example, an OD intervention aimed at a problem of high absenteeism among students would start by finding out how much was known about the problem. It would be important to know if information regarding exact numbers of absent students, times of day, times of week, times of year, and reasons were available. Second, it would be important to know how easily this information could be obtained. That step would be more difficult, but it would be necessary to determine if the information available was all that was necessary to propose constructive solutions. Finally, before anything was done, it would be necessary to check the accuracy and consistency of the information. The role of information in organization development is so important that many OD interventions are primarily information gathering and checking interventions (Nadler, 1977).

Functional Criteria

Functional criteria are the criteria used for decision making and evaluation. Decisions are not looked upon as good or bad but how *functional* they are. Something is considered functional if it advances the organization toward its goals and something is considered dysfunctional if it does not contribute to goal-achievement or if it hinders an organization from reaching its goals. This may seem like mere semantics at first, but it tends to increase the use of valid and objective information in decision making since nothing deserves either a functional or dysfunctional label without determining the role it plays in the organization.

Choices and Commitments

The final key points in OD are informed choices and personal commitments. OD stresses that first of all people should have the opportunity to make *real* choices. Second, people should have sufficient valid information to make well informed choices. This is to say that the choices people make should be significant and that once they decide, their decisions should not be open to arbitrary disregard. Making informed choices has two beneficial outcomes. The first is that people feel involved and more inclined to support decisions they participated in making, especially if they feel they were based on a good appraisal of the situation. The second benefit is related to the first—people can be expected to make commitments to courses of action they helped develop (Argyris, 1970; Belasco and Alutto, 1972; Bridge, 1976; Levine, Derr, Junghans, 1972). Committed staff members can be expected to support programs and to work harder to make them succeed (Berman and McLaughlin, 1978).

OD in Practice

The practice of organization development takes many forms so that no one short presentation can be expected to adequately cover the spectrum. With this in mind, it was decided to describe some of what has been done in the Participative Option Development (POD) project which has been a successful operation since 1973. During this time, the district in which the project is located has sponsored or directed literally dozens of OD efforts. In addition, the approach taken to OD by the project is orthodox and provides a model of OD illustrative of the major aspects of most organization development.

POD Process Model for Change (Martin, Roark, and Tonso, 1978b)

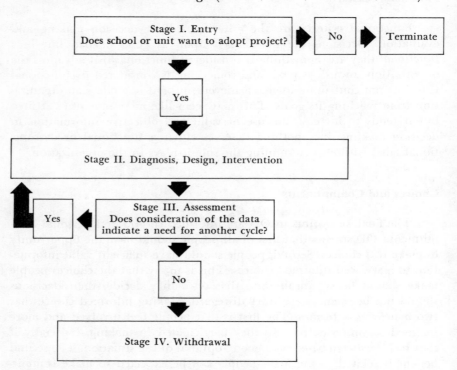

This model of OD consists of four stages with the second stage having three distinct steps. This model was adopted because it is flexible and allows outside consultants, district personnel, and the target personnel to use it.

Stage I. Entry

To a certain extent, all personnel employing OD must achieve entry. Obviously, people not a part of the unit where the OD is being performed have a more difficult task; but it is still basically the same process. A consultant employed in an OD project, a principal doing OD, or any other person basically charged with the operation of an OD program needs to accomplish three tasks in order to achieve entry.

The first task is to gain acceptance. All persons identified with the OD effort must achieve personal acceptance. The most critical elements in this acceptance are credibility and trust. Credibility primarily pertains to capabilities to carry out the functions or effort. Trust primarily pertains to goals and interests. Organization development participants must feel that what is being done is for their benefit and not someone else's. Acceptance also refers to the entire concept of OD. Any organization involved must recognize and, to a certain extent, understand OD as potentially beneficial to the organization. Therefore, acceptance is a twofold operation involving both people and procedure. Knowing when acceptance is achieved is extremely difficult and can only be determined by subjective judgment. This judgment is generally based on little evidence. Often the participant's use of the words "we" and "us" to include the OD personnel and the participant's perception that OD is a high priority activity are the only available evidence.

The second essential task is to develop and use a two-way, valid, accurate, and adequate communication throughout the life of an OD intervention. This communication must be established between OD personnel and the participants, as well as among all persons involved. This is a difficult task since frequently communication may be a major problem of the unit participating in OD (Knobleck and Goldstein, 1971; Robert, 1974). Nevertheless, adequate communication levels are essential for a successful intervention. Process consultation, participant observation, and questionnaires are all techniques that can be used to determine the adequacy of the communication. Failure to determine the level of communication can lead to serious problems. One of the authors once arranged a series of workshops by talking to only one representative of a school district. In defense of the author, he was young and it seemed like a straightforward request made by a knowledgeable administrator in the district office. However, district communication and politics were such that only half of those involved in the school understood what was to be done the way the author did; the half that shared the author's understanding did not include the principal. Serious insinuations and accusations that people had been deliberately misinformed to obtain their participation resulted and it was barely possible to get out of the mess. The entire effort almost failed before it got started.

Establishing a working contract is the final task that must be accomplished. This contract is a complex requirement. One part of it is primarily an emotional understanding which sets the limits and requirements of the relationships between the OD personnel and participants. The second part of the contract contains the general requirements of the intervention and enough specifics to ensure that all parties understand what will be done and who will do it. For example, items like released time, pay for substitutes and consultants, responsibilities for supplies, training facilities, all need to be agreed on in advance as much as possible. The degree of commitment of the administration and potential participation needs to be determined as clearly as possible. Finally, the people responsible for future plans need to be identified and specific plans for the intervention initiated. Most OD failures are probably due to inadequate entry.

Stage II. Diagnosis, Design, Intervention

Once entry has been successfully completed, the OD process enters Stage II.

Step 1—Diagnosis. The first step in Stage II, diagnosis, starts with data collected in the earliest phases of entry. Even the contemplation of OD is generally based on some data; the actual decision to do OD and the specifics are always based, at least partially, on data. The diagnosis phase simply emphasizes the need for information and stimulates gathering information more than any other phase (Fox and others, 1973; Merry and Allerhand, 1977) .

Data collection at this time proceeds through many channels simultaneously. Normally, there is a great deal of informal data gathering based on casual conversations and chance observations. Formal interviews, both structured and unstructured, are common. Questionnaires are perhaps the most common means of gathering normative and comparative information. Meetings and examination of records are also employed frequently (see the case studies at the end of this chapter) .

The focus of this information-gathering activity is generally on finding out what the situation is, how people feel about it, and what situation they desire. The information gathered seldom answers these questions directly and generally requires extensive synthesis and analysis before it is really useful (Merry and Allerhand, 1977; Nadler, 1977) .

In a small school district with an attendance problem, they first examined attendance records to determine the exact nature of the problem. Then they discussed the findings with everyone involved. At this point, they knew what the situation was and how people felt about it. They continued the discussions and determined what people wanted. Since they did not have a plan that promised to improve the situation significantly, a careful study was made of other district policies before a new policy was suggested. This new policy was subsequently adopted. Synthesis and analysis frequently require more information and very often point out serious deficiencies in available data. If the data needed can be gathered, it should be done as soon as possible; if not, making a note of the deficiency for future action is helpful. Ideally, the information should be analyzed in collaboration between consultants and participants but often it is necessary that an OD consultant perform some of the tasks that require specialized skills. Analysis may be done with the assistance of a computer or by simply going over the results and trying to determine their meaning.

Once the data have been analyzed and arranged in an understandable manner, they are made available to all members of the group involved in the OD effort. The purpose in making the data available to all involved is to have everyone take part in the diagnosis. Even personnel not directly involved in the OD activities should be invited to share the information. In essence, two sets of information will be provided. One set concerns what the current situation is and how people feel about it. The other set concerns what participants desire the situation to be. Diagnosis basically involves answering two questions: why aren't we where we want to be? and, what can be done to move to where we want to be? Having the people involved believe the answers to these two questions is one of the main resasons for involving everyone in the diagnosis. It is comparatively easy to disregard what other people tell us is wrong. But, if we decide, for example, that we need better grading practices, we are more likely to do something about it.

Step 2—Design. It is essential that the design be accepted by most of the group so that any interventions carried out will be accepted and supported by the group. The design is used to plan the activities which will be used to move in the desired direction.

In summary, a diagnosis is basically a concise statement of the current situation and what people desire instead. This statement is used to design activities which will move the organization in the desired direction (Doak, 1970; Huse, 1975) .

Step 3—Intervention. There are a number of types of interventions employed in OD (Fordyce and Weil, 1971; French and Bell, 1973; Huse, 1975; Schmuck and Miles, 1971; Schmuck and others, 1977). One of the most common is survey feedback. Basically survey feedback involves surveying people about the situation and giving the results back to those who will make the decisions and implement plans developed. In essence, this is normally done during analysis but it doesn't alter the fact that survey feedback in itself is a powerful intervention (Bowers, 1973; Nadler, 1977). Procedural changes are often suggested as the way to improve the situation. These procedural changes cover a multitude of areas from the classroom to the community and very often include inservice education as a means of implementing recommended changes. Structural changes or reorganization are also recommended frequently. Training or education regarding how the organization (school) functions is a common recommendation. Meetings to improve working and personal relations and to solve specific problems are almost always recommended. Goal setting is also a frequent recommendation.

Stage III. Assessment

Assessment has two objectives. The first is to determine the impact of the intervention and the second is to assess the overall state of the organization. Assessing the impact of the intervention is relatively simple if the groundwork was laid at the beginning of the intervention and often the overall condition of the organization can be determined by the same assessment. For more thorough explanation see Chapter 5 on Evaluating Staff Development. The overall purpose of the assessment is to determine the efficacy of the intervention and to provide indications of the desirability of further OD interventions.

Stage IV. Withdrawal

The withdrawal stage generally involves dissengagement of OD personnel from the client organization. But it often involves reassigning duties and establishing liaison arrangements for continued contact after the formal intervention is completed.

Targets of Organization Development

The most useful way to put organization development into perspective may be to look at its targets. In the attempt to develop more effective ways of organizational functioning, the first target is generally the fit between goals and procedures; the second target is often the freedom/

constraint issue present in any organization. This issue centers on the tension between individual autonomy and organizational constraints. This tension is inevitable; individuals strive for autonomy and the organization strives for control. If there is too much constraint, individual creativity and intelligence are stifled. OD struggles to achieve an optimal balance. The third target is generally the fit between the task and process. The fourth overall target is the amount and quality of data and the related questions of informed choices and commitment (Argyris, 1970; Weisborg, 1977).

These examples may help put the targets into perspective. Telling teachers to become more professional is inappropriate if the goal is to have teachers become more professional. And teaching writing skills by lecture discussion is not likely to succeed. Too much constraint and unprofessional treatment was the cry when one small school district put in time clocks for teachers. Administrators in another district joke about their central administration dress code and violate it in ingenious ways. Showing movies to classes of 30 when an auditorium is available and the schedule could be easily modified to show the movies to a larger group is an example of poor task/process fit. Or consider the fairly common practice of arbitrarily shuffling principals among schools without a plan or their involvement in the decision.

In addition to these four overall targets, OD usually addresses at least six other specific issues. These six issues are the adequacy and appropriateness of (a) leadership, (b) decision making, (c) problem solving, (d) conflict management, (e) communication, and (f) planning (Schmuck and others, 1977). The four targets and these six issues are addressed by OD in an effort to improve the quality of life in the organization and at the same time improve organizational effectiveness. OD approaches these areas without a prescription of how the organization should function, but instead with the philosophy that people with sufficient valid information and freedom of choice have the capacity to improve their lot and their organizational effectiveness (Andrews and Greenfield, 1966-67).

In these six specific areas, as well as in the four general target areas, some research exists which indicates that certain methods achieve more desirable results than others; but the purpose of OD is not to say, "do it this way." Instead, training may be conducted to enhance participants' awareness of the options available to them and of what they can expect by following certain procedures. The purpose of this training is primarily awareness, although skill building is an objective at times.

OD Case Studies

The following examples of OD in schools are presented to bridge the gap between theory and practice and to show how the blend of OD and staff development occurs in practice. The examples are all taken verbatim from the Participative Option Development Project (POD) (Martin, Roark, and Tonso, 1978b) .

The impetus for POD began in 1970 when a districtwide committee was formed to examine the functioning of junior high schools. In 1973, another committee was established to assess needs for optional programs for secondary students. Members of this districtwide Options Committee, composed of administrators, counselors, teachers, students, and parents, designed the POD project. Title IV-C funding was obtained in 1974 for POD.

A number of activities were scheduled in the spring of 1974 to introduce the district staff to OD, including a full-day workshop for secondary principals and counselors, and a university graduate-credit course. All secondary schools were invited to send teacher-counselor-principal teams to the course. Each of the nine teams electing to take the class conducted activities in their own school to explain OD and to determine faculty support for becoming a project pilot school. Four schools applied for pilot school status. Meanwhile, discussions and demonstration events served to secure district and building administrative understanding and support for the project.

POD has engaged in a number of activities in addition to working with the four pilot schools. These activities ranged from the formation of a district OD cadre to mini-interventions which lasted only a few days.

Cadre (Peaceful Valley)*

The POD Project Staff trained 20 district teachers, counselors, administrators, and parents as part-time OD specialists. Beginning in March 1976, this group learned skills in interpersonal communication, group processes, consultation, and other aspects of OD. By the spring of 1977, the POD Cadre began extensive field work.

Presently, POD Cadre members consult with school groups to improve the ways school groups work together to solve shared problems and reach shared goals. Teams of Cadre members have assisted a variety of schools and groups within the district in a number of activities ranging from data gathering to planning effective parent group meetings. A few

* Fictitious name.

examples of Cadre activities include (1) designing strategies to improve working relationships among members of a secondary school department, (2) planning a survey of community attitudes toward a secondary school, (3) identifying faculty goals and determining ways the principal could assist the faculty in reaching the goals, and (4) training parents as group discussion leaders for a workshop in which parents identified budget priorities for an elementary school.

Assistance from the Cadre begins with a request from a school for a meeting to discuss the relationship between the school "wants" and the Cadre services. The Cadre team and a school committee become a Planning Team to decide upon goals and procedures for the intervention. The Planning Team then collects pertinent data and designs the intervention to meet specific needs identified through analyzing the data.

Examples of services which the POD Cadre provides district schools include the following:

Diagnosis—using questionnaires, interviews, and other methods to get information for making decisions about concerns or needs.

Skills Training—teaching skills in communication, problem solving, decision making, and other interpersonal skills.

Leadership Consultation—working with leaders to conduct short, productive meetings; to improve the ways the group works together, and to identify major goals.

Planning—identifying problems and goals and designing systematic procedures to reach the goals and solve the problems.

Team-Building—building interpersonal relationships, managing conflict, setting goals, and improving team cooperation.

From January 1977 through February 1978, trained Cadre members were involved in approximately 35 interventions. The numbers of Cadre members involved in each intervention have ranged from one person for a one-to-one consultation to five Cadre members for facilitation or training of groups of up to 100 people. In one instance, nine Cadre members planned and facilitated a workshop on competency-based testing for the Board of Education, the Accountability Committee, and representative district leadership personnel. The length of time involved in Cadre interventions has ranged from a few hours to several months.

Beginning in February 1978, Cadre members served as trainers for a group of potential Cadre members. As in the first Cadre training class, participants applied as school teams consisting of a principal, counselor, and teachers. From approximately 70 applicants, 49 were selected. The teams represent seven elementary schools, three secondary schools, and central office. Participants finishing the three phase training program in January 1979, became new members of the Cadre team.

The Cadre continues to function and at present the POD staff is conducting Cadre training for another public school system, the largest in the state. This district plans to use its Cadre in much the same way that it has functioned in Peaceful Valley.

Mini Intervention (Paintbrush* Elementary School, 1977)

Entry. In the spring, the Board of Education and the Central Administration requested building principals to involve faculty and parent representatives in developing the building budget for the coming school year. The principal at Paintbrush Elementary School requested assistance from the POD Cadre in developing an action plan to obtain a maximum amount of parent and staff input for setting budget priorities.

Diagnosis. Three Cadre members worked as a team to assist in planning and carrying out the action plan. During the initial contact, the expectations of the principal and role of the Cadre were clarified. Formal diagnostic procedures were unnecessary since the task was clear.

Design. The Cadre team met to plan strategies for involving school and community members during implementation of the action plan. The Cadre team then met with the principal to develop a tentative agenda for a community meeting in which community members and school staff would collaborate in setting budget priorities. The community meeting was structured to utilize parent-teacher teams as discussion leaders for small groups. The principal and the Cadre team then met with the parent-teacher teams to discuss and modify the agenda. The parent-teacher teams identified their tasks for the community meeting and were also trained in group process facilitation. The principal and Cadre team met a few days before the community meeting to review handouts, discuss presentations, and allocate time to the agenda items.

Intervention. At the community meeting, the principal presented the building allocation and a history of budget priorities within the school. Community members and school staff were then randomly assigned to parent-teacher discussion leaders and each group met to develop a list of their perceptions of school needs. Each list was refined and synthesized to eliminate duplication and to cluster common items in order of priority. At the close of the meeting, each group posted a final list and reported its priorities to the total group. Participants viewed each group's list

* Fictitious name.

while refreshments were served. During the meeting, a Cadre member acted as facilitator and process observer.

Withdrawal. A steering committee composed of parents and faculty synthesized the lists from each group and developed six major need areas for the school. After meeting with the principal to assess the effectiveness of the community meeting, the Cadre team withdrew from the school.

Conclusion. The entire process from Entry to Withdrawal took one month, during which seven events occurred involving the principal and the Cadre team. The primary Cadre contribution to the project was planning activities and agendas and training group leaders. Subsequently, the principal asked Cadre members to work with building task forces to develop action plans to meet the six major need areas of the school.

Goals of OD in Schools

It is difficult to specify what the main goal for organization development is in schools. It is easy to say that the goals are self-renewing schools, responsive schools, or effective education. But, it is hard to say what these terms mean and even harder to know when they have been accomplished. Nevertheless, these are probably the goals of OD as practiced by most people in public schools.

The relative order of importance of these goals and the method of formulating them would undoubtedly vary considerably among OD practitioners but no one is likely to object to any of the three. In order of abstractness, or breadth of coverage, effective education is too broad a concept to provide useful direction.

The concept of self-renewing schools is somewhat more precise but it, too, lacks the precision needed for setting objectives, designing activities, or evaluating outcomes.

The responsive school idea is somewhat more precise since we can specify *how* schools are supposed to be responsive. Theoretically, responsive schools react positively to (a) change, (b) needs of students, faculty, and community; and (c) tension in all facets of the educational process.

The jury is still out on whether OD actually enhances the responsiveness of schools or whether it is better than other techniques for doing so in actual practice. Research in the area is still meager although it is improving (Marguilies, Wright, and Scholl, 1977; Morrison, 1978; Pate, Nielsen, and Bacon, 1977). In fact, research cannot tell us unequivocably whether OD works or not. What we have is considerable evidence that OD does work and that it works in developing responsive schools (Alschuler, 1972; Keutzer and others, 1971; Keys and Kreisman, 1978).

In summary, staff development and OD both work to improve schools and ultimately education, but from somewhat different perspectives. Staff development attempts to achieve its goals primarily through an increase in individual competence while OD concentrates on organizational competence. Both strive to improve the lot of both teachers and students and to improve the quality of education as a whole. In the process of working to achieve their goals, both methods ultimately affect both the individuals and the organization. One complements the other; they function well side by side.

REFERENCES

Alschuler, A. "Toward a Self Renewing School." *The Journal of Applied Behavioral Science* 8 (1972) : 577-600.

Andrews, J. H., and Greenfield, J. B. "Organizational Themes Relevant to Change in Schools." *Ontario Journal of Educational Research* 9 (1966-67) : 81-99.

Argyris, C. *Intervention Theory and Method*. Reading, Mass.: Addison-Wesley, 1970.

Belasco, J. A., and Alutto, J. A. "Decisional Participation and Teacher Participation." *Educational Administration Quarterly* 8 (1972) : 44-58.

Berman, P., and McLaughlin, M. W. "Federal Programs Supporting Educational Change." *Implementing and Sustaining Innovations*. Washington, D.C.: U.S. Office of Education, R-1589 No. 8—HEW, 1978.

Bowers, D. G. "OD Techniques and Their Results in 23 Organizations: The Michigan ICL Study." *The Journal of Applied Behavioral Science* 9 (1973) : 21-43.

Bridge, R. G. "Parent Participation in School Innovations." *Teachers College Record* 77 (1976) : 366-384.

Davis, Keith. *Human Behavior at Work—Human Relations and Organizational Behavior*. New York: McGraw-Hill, 1972.

Doak, E. D. "Organizational Climate: Prelude to Change." *Educational Leadership* 27 (1970) : 367-371.

Filmore, W. J. "What is O.D.—No More Definitions, Please." *O.D. Practitioner* (1974) : 1-2.

Fordyce, J. K., and Weil, R. *Managing with People*. Reading Mass.: Addison-Wesley, 1971.

Fox, R. S., et al. "School Climate Improvement: A Challenge to the School Administrator." *Phi Delta Kappan* (1973) .

French, W. L. and Bell, C. *Organization Development*. Englewood Cliffs, N.J.: Prentice-Hall, 1973.

Hess, F., and Greenstein, G. "Organizational Development: An Idea Whose Time Has Come." *Educational Technology* 12 (1972) : 57-60.

Horning, R.; Metzdorf, J.; and Schiff, S. *Staff Development Academy: Professional Growth Program*. Lakewood, Colo.: Jefferson County Schools, Fall 1979.

Hoy, W. K., and Miskel, C. G. *Educational Administration: Theory, Research and Practice*. New York: Random House, 1978.

Huse, E. *Organization Development and Change*. New York: West, 1975.

Katz, D. M., and Kahn, R. L. *The Social Psychology of Organizations*. New York: John Wiley, 1978.

Keutzer, S.; Fosmire, F. R.; Diller, R.; and Smith, M. D. "Laboratory Training in a New Social System: Evaluation of a Consulting Relationship with High School Faculty." *The Journal of Applied Science* 7 (1971) : 493-501.

Keys, B., and Kreisman, R. L. "Organization Development, Classroom Climate, and Grade Level." *Group and Organization Studies* 3 (1978) : 224-238.

Knobleck, P., and Goldstein, A. P. *The Lonely Teacher.* Boston: Allyn and Bacon, 1971.

Levine, D. M.; Derr, C. B.; and Junghans, R. P. "Educational Planning with Organizational Development: A People-Involving Approach to Systematic Planning." *Educational Technology* 12 (1972) : 14-30.

Marguilies, N.; Wright, P. L.; and Scholl, R. W. "Organization Techniques: Their Impact on Change." *Group and Organization Studies* 2 (1977) : 428-448.

Martin, L.; Roark, A. E.; and Tonso, C. *Participative Option Development: Adoption Manual.* Boulder, Colo.: ESEA Title IV, Part C, 1978a.

Martin, L.; Roark, A. E.; and Tonso, C. *Participative Option Development: Adoption Manual.* Boulder, Colo.: ESEA Title IV, Part C., 1978b.

Merry, V., and Allerhand, M. E. *Developing Teams and Organizations: A Practical Handbook for Managers and Consultants.* Reading, Mass.: Addison-Wesley, 1977.

Morrison, P. "Evaluation in OD: A Review and an Assessment," *Group and Organization Studies* 3 (1978) : 42-69.

Nadler, D. A. *Feedback and Organization Development: Using Data-Based Methods.* Reading, Mass.: Addison-Wesley, 1977.

Pate, L. E.; Neilsen, W. R.; and Bacon, P. C. "Advances in Research in Organization Development: Toward a Beginning." *Group and Organization Studies* 2 (1977) : 449-460.

Robert, M. *Loneliness in the Schools.* Niles, Ill.: Argus, 1974.

Schmuck, R., and Miles, M., eds. *Organization Development in Schools.* Palo Alto, Calif.: National Pass Books, 1971.

Schmuck, R.; Runkel, P. J.; Arends, J. H.; and Arends, R. I. *The Second Handbook of Organization Development in Schools.* Palo Alto, Calif.: Mayfield, 1977.

Stewart, B. "What is Organizational Development and How Does it Apply to Schools?" *Education Canada* 13 (1973) : 19-21.

Weisborg, M. R. "How Do You Know it Works if You Don't Know What it is?" *O.D. Practitioner* 9 (1977) : 1-8.

Weisborg, M. R. "Organizational Diagnosis: Six Places to Look for Trouble With or Without Theory." *Group and Organization Studies* 1 (1976) : 430-447.

4

Designing Effective Staff Development Programs
Fred H. Wood, Steven R. Thompson, and Sister Frances Russell

APPROACHING THE GENERAL PROBLEM of designing staff development systems, Fred Wood, Steven Thompson, and Sister Frances Russell provide a statement of beliefs or assumptions on which they operate, present a five-stage process for creating and initiating inservice systems, and give examples of the operation of their process in schools.

Their goal is to generate an environment which meets organizational and individual needs, and has the ability to modify itself as perceived needs and conditions change. Thus, staff development cannot be "in place" and static. It needs to pulse gently in tune with the lives of professionals and the organizations in which they work. The approach described here represents one way of synthesizing knowledge about organizations, organizational change, and training into a coherent paradigm for constructing programs.

The work ahead of us is to build flowing systems of staff development which help educators enrich their lives and competence, faculties improve their schools, and school systems initiate curricular and organizational changes. Until *systems* of staff development are pervasive, implementing *ad hoc* programs will be the norm.

THE BEST POSSIBLE UNDERGRADUATE preparation for teachers or graduate education for administrators and supervisors cannot serve professionals adequately for more than five to seven years in this age of rapid change and expanding knowledge. The moment educators leave their training institutions they embark upon a journey toward obsolescence (Rubin, 1975). Somehow educators must keep up with the new knowledge and technology in their areas of specialization.

The military, health services, and industry all recognize this need for continuous growth and make extensive use of inservice education for their personnel. The armed services of this country require men and women to up-date their knowledge and skills constantly through carefully ordered and monitored educational programs. The medical field, through specialty boards and medical centers, provides seminars and workshops for physicians, nurses, and others in the health-related services; some specializations require yearly postgraduate work. Businesses, such as American Telephone and Telegraph, IBM, and General Motors have elaborate training centers, while others spend substantial sums of money to send their personnel to universities and private training centers (Wagstaff and McCullough, 1973).

Educators also recognize the need for continuous inservice education of teachers, and, to a lesser extent, of administrators, supervisors, and others in elementary and secondary schools. However, as reported by Joyce and Dillon-Peterson in their chapters, staff development efforts of educators are generally ineffective and poorly conceived, lacking a conceptual framework. Often those responsible for staff growth ignore the available learning theory and research when designing and implementing training programs for teachers and administrators. Educators need a clear concept of inservice that enables them to design and conduct more effective staff development programs. As Rubin (1975) puts it, we need to define the attributes and plan the mechanisms for effective inservice education.

It is critical that the design of inservice education for elementary and secondary school personnel be grounded in our best practice and research. The last two decades have provided substantial data that can serve as the basis for designing inservice. Our best sources come from research, literature, and practice in the areas of staff development and inservice education, adult learning and development, and organization development; all discussed earlier in this yearbook. Research and practice in the area of education change, leader behavior, teacher training, and supervision also add significantly to our view of how to design inservice programs.

This chapter presents a framework for designing inservice staff development programs, based upon an analysis of the available theory, research, and best practice related to inservice education. Included in the authors' view of how to plan inservice that has a significant and lasting effect on educational practice and student outcomes are: (1) a set of assumptions about schools, school personnel, and staff development; (2) a five-stage model of inservice education; and (3) a set of characteristics to guide the design of effective inservice education programs. When possible, practical examples from current inservice programs in public schools are reported, to bridge theory and practice.

We will tend to refer to teachers when talking about inservice; however, the reader should remember that the ideas presented are equally applicable to administrators and others professionals in the schools.

Assumptions That Shape the Inservice Model

There are a variety of ways to view people, schools, and change that affect how inservice is designed, delivered, and assessed. Some educators view inservice as a way of implementing districtwide change and goals; others believe inservice should address teacher needs. Some view inservice as a way of eliminating weaknesses in teachers or principals; others see inservice as developmental or professional growth. Some see inservice as a way of helping educators do their present jobs more effectively; others think inservice should be based upon personal needs and interests of teachers or administrators. There is little doubt that to understand and use any organizational framework for inservice education, one must be aware of the assumptions that undergird it. Different assumptions lead to very different approaches to planning staff growth.

The approach to designing inservice that will be presented here is shaped by a number of assumptions. Most of these assumptions have support from research; all appear to be common to successful inservice programs. Before proceeding, it seems appropriate to present the beliefs that have guided the development of our five-stage approach to inservice education.

1. *All personnel in schools, to stay current and effective, need and should be involved in inservice throughout their careers.* Staff development should continue from the first days educators enter a teaching position until they retire or leave education. Teachers, administrators, and university personnel support required participation in ongoing inservice (Joyce and Peck, 1977). Teachers become master teachers after they have been employed and working with children. The same might be said for master administrators, supervisors, and counselors.

2. *Significant improvement in educational practice takes considerable time and is the result of systematic, long-range staff development.* Educators constantly look for instant success, immediate improvements in professional performance and student achievement. However, inservice is effective when short term workshops, classroom supervision, and other staff development activities are viewed as a part of a larger effort to achieve a significant change in current practice. Instant changes in professional behavior are unlikely to be significant; seldom are they lasting.

3. *Inservice education should have an impact on the quality of the school program and focus on helping staff improve their abilities to perform their professional responsibilities* (Hart, 1974; Wagstaff and McCullough, 1973; Ernst, 1974; Edelfelt, 1977). While professional development needs to include both those activities desired by educators and those needed to perform the role defined in the school program, highest priority should go to improving competencies "to do one's job." Funds for staff development are limited; priorities must be set. Of course, it is

also important that professional duties and roles be developed jointly, that is, teachers should be involved in defining the nature of instructional practices and programs in their school.

4. *Adult learners are motivated to risk learning new behaviors when they believe they have control over the learning situation and are free from threat of failure.* Adult learning is ego involved. Learning a new instructional skill, technique, or concept may promote a positive or negative view of oneself. Fear of external judgment from superiors that we as teachers or administrators may be viewed as less than adequate, especially in learning situations such as those presented in inservice training programs, is always present. To the extent possible, inservice should be structured to avoid the threat and anxiety of failure (Withall and Wood, 1979).

5. *Educators vary widely in their professional competencies, readiness, and approaches to learning.* For inservice programs to be effective, they need to accommodate the individual differences that exist among the teachers and administrators who participate in them. Individualization is essential in effective staff development programs.

6. *Professional growth requires personal and group commitment to new performance norms.* Changes in professional practice start with a desire to behave differently. Adults, to a great extent, make their own decisions about what they will and will not learn; they are the "gate keepers" for what will be learned. Educators are much more likely to be open to new learning when they and their peers have cooperatively developed a commitment to changes in their behavior.

7. *Organizational health including factors such as social climate, trust, open communication, and peer support for change in practice influence the success of professional development programs.* A change in individual behavior requires a supportive environment. Both the individual and the school staff have norms, a personality, and behavior that affect staff development. If the culture of the organization is not healthy, the changes anticipated as the result of inservice usually do not occur (Goodlad, 1975).

8. *The school is the primary unit of change; not the district or the individual* (Goodlad, 1975). Given the size of school districts that serve most students in the United States, it is doubtful whether significant change in practice can be implemented across an entire system (Berman and McLaughlin, 1978). The individual teacher, on the other hand, is too small a unit and too isolated a target for change.

9. *School districts have the primary responsibility for providing the resources and training necessary for a school staff to implement new pro-*

grams and improve instruction. With limited exceptions, time, money, and other resources for staff development are in the hands of the local districts. No other major source is available to support the changes the local district and school staff want. If a district or any institution wants growth and improved performance, it must provide the resources to support the training necessary for the desired improved practice to occur.

10. *The school principal is the gatekeeper for adoption and continued use of new practices and programs in a school* (Berman and McLaughlin, 1978). For staff development to have a lasting effect, the principal must be committed to the implementation of the inservice goals, participate in the inservice planning and activities, encourage other staff members to participate in training programs, and support and reinforce the implementation of new knowledge, skills, and strategies.

11. *Effective inservice programs must be based upon research, theory, and the best education practice.* Those responsible for planning inservice programs need to use what educators and researchers in other fields have learned that relates to staff development. The time when educators could exclusively use gut feelings and conventional wisdom to guide decisions about professional inservice has passed.

In designing this inservice education model, we have tried to be consistent with these beliefs. For those educators who agree with these beliefs, the approach to inservice education described here will seem reasonable and appropriate. For those who are looking for instant change, who believe staff development should be controlled by administrators, who think inservice education is best directed toward districtwide change, or who view inservice as a means to remediate deficiencies in professional practice, our approach will seem inadequate and inappropriate.

To assist the reader, we have been explicit in stating the assumptions that have guided our thinking concerning how inservice should be designed and implemented. First, our beliefs provide a mind-set for thinking about inservice. Second, if one has never examined his or her own beliefs about change, adult learners, professional growth, and school climate as they relate to inservice education, these statements may provide a starting point for self-examination. Finally, to understand the inservice model described here, it is important to be conscious of the assumptions that guided the development of each of the five stages.

Design of a Model for Inservice Education

Inservice education may be viewed as having five distinct but related stages. These stages include Readiness, Planning, Training, Implementation, and Maintenance. Stage I, Readiness, emphasizes selection and understanding of, and commitment to new professional behaviors by a school staff or group of educators. In Stage II, Planning, the specific plans for an inservice program are developed to achieve the desired changes in professional practice selected in Stage I. In the Training Stage, Stage III, the plans are translated into practice. The Implementation Stage, Stage IV, focuses on ensuring that the training becomes part of the ongoing professional behavior of teachers and administrators in their own work setting. Stage V, Maintenance, begins as new behaviors are integrated into daily practice. The aim of this final stage is to ensure that once a change in performance is operational, it will continue over time.

While these stages are discrete and tend to be sequential, they are part of an ongoing, overlapping cycle of inservice education. For example, the Readiness Stage occurs primarily during the first year of a four or five year inservice cycle. However, during each year some attention is given to readiness, although emphasis on Stage I activities decreases after the early months of the cycle. Planning is also emphasized in the first eight to twelve months of the cycle, but some planning will occur each year of an inservice program. This same pattern of overlap is also evident in the other three stages.

Within each stage, the source of leadership and the amount of direction provided by the leader vary. The degree to which decisions are shared, or in the hands of those in authority, or made by those who are expected to change their behavior should be based upon *expertise rather than position*. Since leadership in inservice programs is crucial and since leadership demands vary, we will attempt to clarify this issue as we discuss each stage.

Another topic that will be addressed briefly in each of the five stages is the formative and summative data that need to be collected.* In the early stages, the emphasis will be on data necessary to assist those responsible for designing and implementing inservice programs in making appropriate decisions about the inservice plan. Since Chapter 5 deals with evaluating inservice education, only the kinds of data to be collected at each relevant stage will be discussed.

Stage I: Readiness

Readiness is the crucial, but most often forgotten, stage in the design of staff development programs. A school climate that supports change in professional behavior is developed in this stage. In this initial period, the school staff identifies possible solutions to instructional and programmatic problems. Readiness also includes selecting specific programs, processes, and procedures to be used in a school. At this point, individual and group commitments to and understandings of the desired changes in professional behaviors are established.

Mobilizing Support

Throughout this early stage of planning inservice programs, the focus is on mobilizing broad-based support for changes in professional practice and for the staff development necessary to implement those changes. This support is obtained through the involvement of teachers, principals, central office staff, school board members, and, when possible, parents. Participation of some central office staff and the principal is particularly important to demonstrate administrative support for the decisions that are made. Their involvement also enables central office personnel and principals to understand why a faculty decides to make particular changes. Parent involvement builds understanding and support for program changes and inservice education on the part of the public. Research by the Rand Corporation indicates that for changes in school practice to occur and last, this broad-based involvement is essential (Berman and McLaughlin, 1978).

The first task in getting a school staff ready to change their professional performance is to develop a school climate where communications are clear and open, where the faculty knows each other well and understands each other's professional values, where the teachers and administrators trust and support each other, and where the faculty sees differences among their peers as strengths. In this climate, educators are ready to solve problems and to develop a common set of expectations about goals for improvement that can guide inservice education. Seldom do most administrators conceive of a school as an organic, goal-oriented unit that is the target for norms, values, and behaviors that must change (Blumberg, 1976). Yet, it is precisely this view that guides the Readiness Stage.

During Stage I, stress is on creating new expectations for teachers and administrators, new group behaviors, and new commitments to changes in how one carries out his or her professional role. For example, through the use of structured activities, a school faculty may build

* Simply stated, formative data provide information that enables those responsible for staff development to determine whether the inservice plans, procedures, activities, and materials are being implemented and how those plans, procedures, activities, and materials might be modified to increase their effectiveness. Summative data are concerned with assessing the effects of the inservice program (and its components) once it is in final form.

relationships, identify significant instructional and curriculum problems to be solved, set goals for their school program, and select specific changes in practice that they believe ought to be implemented over the next three to five years. During this process, teachers and administrators commit themselves to new but shared norms for professional behavior, first as individuals and then as a group.

Since it is difficult to commit to unfamiliar practices and programs, it is necessary to spend some time during this stage becoming aware of the possibilities. What are the most promising programs, materials, strategies, or skills being used by other educators in similar settings? Are there research data that can help in the selection of new professional behaviors to solve local problems or improve current practice? What are some staff members in the school doing that the rest of the staff should do? Awareness of these kinds of things helps assure that decisions and commitments made at this point are based upon knowledge about available options.

Leadership

The leadership and initiative for Readiness come primarily from central office personnel in cooperation with the principal of a school. Any limits to the areas of improvement that must be addressed—for example, the state's mandate to mainstream handicapped children—are identified and made public prior to involving the total school staff. While the decisions about the specific changes the faculty will implement are made by the principal and teachers, the readiness activities are usually planned and implemented by administrators with the assistance of personnel who are skilled in directing organizational development and growth.

The Stage I Plan

The results of the Readiness Stage are (1) a written set of inservice goals (desired changes in professional behavior) that the faculty of a school helps select, understands, and is committed to implement, (2) a description of the specific programs and practices selected to achieve these goals, and (3) a broad, very general four-to-five year plan for implementing the desired change in the ongoing program. Evaluation data are collected to determine the extent to which the goals, programs, practices, and general plan are understood and supported by the school staff. In addition, data can be collected prior to, during, and after this stage to assess the climate of the school.

While attention to getting faculty ready for inservice training in the manner we have described through the use of organization development strategies has been limited in public schools, there are examples that can help clarify these processes. The Churchill Area School District in suburban Pittsburgh and the Staff Development Center of the Ferguson-Florissant School District in suburban St. Louis have both emphasized this stage in designing their inservice programs. In each district, the central office staff is committed to inservice education and decentralized, school-by-school program improvement. They also believe that school faculties should be involved in defining how they will improve current practice.

To define the areas of and goals for their inservice programs, both districts used a workshop developed by the Institute for the Development of Educational Activities (/I/D/E/A/), a division of the Charles F. Kettering Foundation. During this three-day workshop called "We Agree," the teachers, principals, central office staff, and parents spend about 14 hours in groups of five to seven participating in a series of organization development activities. These structured activities help the faculty become better acquainted, clarify their values related to issues concerning teaching and working in schools, and improve their communication and problem-solving skills. During the final eight to ten hours of the sessions, the participants used problem-solving and consensus-seeking skills acquired during the first 14 hours to develop shared belief statements about what their school should be like. Statements were prepared on their instructional program, how students learn, school organization, teacher-student relationships, and school, community, and parent relationships.

These statements were then used as guidelines to determine which practices in their schools were appropriate and should be used by more of the faculty and which were inappropriate. In addition, a task force of school staff used these statements to establish goals for new practices and programs. Based upon visits to other schools, use of consultants, attendance at conferences, and, in some cases, participation in simulations where teachers and administrators tried out new approaches to instruction with students, the staff of each school selected the changes they wanted to implement over the next four years. For the Churchill School, the final product was a plan for a new middle school program. Some of the schools in the Ferguson-Florissant District used the process to identify areas of improvement for their school; others developed a more comprehensive plan such as Churchill's. Throughout this process every effort was made to select the goals and changes by consensus so all who were to change their behavior had some commitment to that change.

Once a school has established a climate conducive to growth, developed common expectations for improvement, and made a commitment to professional development, it is ready to move on to Stage II.

Stage II: Planning

According to teachers, administrators, and university professors, a major defect in inservice education programs has been poor organization and planning (Joyce and Peck, 1977). The design of inservice programs is the focus of the Planning Stage where the goals and programs selected in the previous stage are translated into a detailed, long-range plan for staff development. During this stage, the goals are refined into specific inservice objectives; a needs assessment is conducted; inservice activities are planned; resources are identified; and the tentative design—the who, how, what, when, and where—of the Training and Implementation Stages are identified.

Inservice Objectives

Inservice education should be based upon clear, specific objectives that are congruent with the goals and programs selected by teachers and administrators in Stage I. These objectives identify three essentials: (1) knowledge, (2) strategies and skills, and (3) attitudes required to implement the improvements desired by a school faculty (Rubin, 1975). In any effort to improve instruction or school practice, there is a need to consider inservice outcomes in all three areas. Inservice objectives are the result of careful analysis of the goals and programs to be implemented and research findings related to those outcomes and programs.

Knowledge objectives deal with learning and using specific content. For example, current efforts to introduce metrics and nutrition into the public school curriculum demand that many teachers develop content knowledge in these subject areas to enable them to teach the appropriate concepts and principles.

Strategies or skill objectives pertain to new procedures for teaching such as how to plan, manage, and evaluate independent study, contract learning, small group instruction, or inquiry teaching. For administrators, these objectives might deal with how to conduct classroom observations using clinical supervision or systematic observation schedules.

Attitude objectives identify the commitments, values, and other affective variables necessary to implement change in professional behavior.

Teachers, for example, must be willing to let students take on the responsibility of planning some of their own learning if independent study is to be effective; or they must believe that they can individualize instruction before they will use a diagnostic approach to teaching mathematics. Administrators must trust teachers and value their involvement to use clinical supervision techniques that allow teachers to select areas where they will improve their instruction.

Needs Assessment

.   Once specific objectives are identified, those responsible for planning inservice programs need to determine which outcomes should be addressed. This is done through a needs assessment, a device for identifying gaps between what "should be" and what "is" in current practice.

There are a variety of ways to determine discrepancies between expectations defined in the inservice objectives and practice. Often, a questionnaire is used to ask teachers and administrators what they need or want to improve. In some cases the same questionnaire is completed by the teachers and the principal. The teachers indicate which outcomes they wish to pursue and the principal rates each teacher in terms of the areas of needed improvement. This provides a check of perceived needs for inservice. Where differences exist, classroom observations and interviews can then be used to verify the needs of individuals and groups of teachers.

One of the most effective means of assessing inservice needs is to interview teachers about the objectives they and their colleagues should focus on during inservice programs. Interviews with teachers and administrators appear to provide the most accurate and honest feedback concerning the objectives where gaps exist between desired and actual competencies. The interview is more personal than the questionnaire and allows those collecting data an opportunity to clarify expressed needs. Respondents tend to take more time and give more consideration to their responses in an interview than they do in responding to a questionnaire (Jones, 1973).

Another helpful method that may be used for identifying inservice needs is nominal grouping (VandeVen and Delbecq, 1974; Ford, 1975). The nominal group process is a highly structured sequence of small group activities designed to regulate interactions. Once the groups are formed and the task is identified, the process follows five steps:

1. *Listing*—participants list their responses to the task; no interaction is permitted

2. *Round-robin*—participants present items from their lists, round-robin fashion, which are recorded for later use; no other interaction is permitted

3. *Voting*—using cards or ballots, each participant ranks the items on the group's master list to show his/her priorities for the items; again, no interaction is allowed

4. *Discussion*—voting results are tabulated and discussed

5. *Final voting*—each participant votes a final time, listing priorities from the master list. The results may then be tabulated and analyzed.

Additional sources for identifying inservice needs include supervisor judgments, external evaluators, and student test data. However, no decisions about needs of teachers or administrators should be made without their involvement. This avoids the problem of having inservice viewed as something done to educators rather than something they do to and for themselves.

Needs assessments also ought to provide information about the learning style of those for whom the inservice program will be planned. Information about individual differences such as when and how one learns best; what learning modes, activities, and rewards are preferred; and how self-directed the participants are in new learning experiences is needed to assure that these important variables are accommodated in the learning activities. This type of data has seldom been collected as part of inservice needs assessment. Yet, it is impossible to individualize staff development without it. The Murdock Teacher Center in Wichita, Kansas, has developed a Student Learning Styles Survey which can be adapted and used to collect this kind of information. Other procedures for assessing learning style have been developed by Anthony Gregorc at the University of Connecticut, Storrs, and by Joseph Hill at Oakland College in Bloomfield Hills, Michigan.

Available Resources

For a successful inservice plan, one must be familiar with available resources and constraints. What staff within the district or school can conduct the inservice training and follow up activities? How much school time can be used for staff development? What funds are available for materials, consultants, and substitutes? Successful inservice education requires administrative support in the form of time, personnel, materials, and funds. Information on resources helps planners set priorities and select activities that are appropriate and feasible.

Planning Inservice Activities

Plans for inservice activities—workshops, visitations, graduate courses, practicums—should include: (1) opportunities to build relationships and communication among the participants; (2) time when participants can interact freely and share what they are learning; (3) pre- and post-assessments; and (4) learning options to accommodate differences in achievement and learning style uncovered in the needs assessment and differences in competence detrimental in the pre-assessment. Of particular importance are on-the-job experiences that can be employed during the Training Stage to assure those in the inservice an oportunity to use and practice what is being learned. The need for hands-on experience in adult learning will be discussed further in the Training Stage.

The plan should also identify the actual materials, inservice staff, consultants, facilities, and equipment that will be used in the workshops or training activity. Care should be taken to select or develop inservice activities and materials and to use facilities that mirror the work setting of the participants. The more participants see that what they are learning works in schools like their own, the more likely they are to use their new skills and understanding back on the job.

Leadership

Leadership and decision making about inservice plans are shared among teachers and administrators. As much as possible, those who will participate in the training should be involved in the decisions about objectives, activities, and assessment. One means of involving teachers in planning is the use of an inservice steering committee for a school. This committee, working with the principal and, when needed, central office personnel or outside consultants, guides the development of the inservice plan for their school. They provide a communication link with the total faculty and eventually monitor the implementation of the plan.

Since most teachers and principals are not prepared to take on the responsibilities of planning inservice programs, there is a need to help the steering committee learn how to design such programs. Thus, in the initial stages, the leadership will need guidance from supervisors or inservice specialists to facilitate appropriate decisions. As a steering committee becomes knowledgeable about the planning process, they can then take over the planning. The key point is that school level personnel will need guided inservice experiences to learn their roles in developing effective staff development programs for their faculty.

The Phase II Plan

As a result of the Planning Stage, a school staff has a written plan for inservice covering as many as five years. The document includes: (1) goals and programs to be implemented; (2) specific inservice objectives to be addressed in the inservice activities; (3) an overall, four- or five-year sequence of activities for training staff and for putting the desired changes in practice; (4) a detailed description of the major inservice workshops and other activities that have been planned for the first 12 to 18 months of the four years; (5) a list of resources—personnel and materials—that can be used to implement the inservice activities; and (6) a budget to support the inservice program and changes in the school program; for example, new textbooks, equipment, or teacher assistants. At this stage, the plan should be evaluated to determine its workability and potential to achieve the desired goals and program changes.

Other Planning Considerations

Some inservice efforts will require that the planning stage include the development of training materials and the selection and field-testing of new curriculum materials and teaching strategies. The need for such products and procedures grows out of the planning of inservice and an analysis of the available resources. If the materials and procedures needed to bring about a desired change are not available or need to be modified before they fit the local needs, then attention should be given to this prior to the start of inservice training. There is a difference between curriculum or materials design and inservice. To focus on both at the same time, as we have in the past, usually results in the design of the curriculum changes but not their implementation. Of course, if one is teaching teachers how to write curriculum, then the inservice should include the development of curriculum materials. Many efforts to change teaching in the school, however, are not focused on development of curriculum but on implementing the instructional implications of a curriculum plan.

The training of local teachers and administrators to conduct the inservice may also occur in this stage. The planners may discover a lack of expertise within the district or school to conduct the inservice activities they've planned. Since the focus is on school level change and leadership, the development of local expertise to conduct inservice promotes peer teaching, reduces the threat of being judged by one's supervisors, and helps provide support personnel during the Implementation Stage.

Stage III: Training

In the Training Stage, the inservice plan is conducted and the content, skills, and attitudes needed to implement the changes in professional behavior are learned. Effective training activities are guided by what is known about adult learning (see Chapter 2). This knowledge shapes the roles of those who direct and those who participate in inservice activities and the nature of the inservice experiences.

While there are many options for inservice—workshops, independent study, sabbaticals, teacher exchange, graduate courses—the primary vehicle for inservice in the public schools has been, and will probably continue to be, the workshop. A workshop can take many forms. In this approach to inservice, a workshop is defined as a group of people participating in structured activities during a specified period of time to accomplish predetermined goals and tasks which lead to new understanding and changes in professional behaviors. In describing the training stage, then, we will focus on the nature of effective workshops; that is, the sequence of experience, options in learning experiences, feedback, leadership roles, and participant responsibilities. While the ideas and principles presented deal with workshops, they also have implications for other inservice modes.

Orientation Activities

The orientation activities in a workshop should provide participants with a clear understanding of inservice objectives, the sequence of activities, expectations and options for the learners, and how the workshop relates to their needs and can help them carry out their day-to-day professional responsibilities. In addition, diagnostic data should be collected about the entry skills of the participants in relation to each of the objectives for the workshop. This kind of information can be obtained through self-assessment questionnaires, formal testing, or observation of those involved during practice activities or back in the work setting. It is also in the orientation session that the theoretical and research base for the training is reviewed.

Learning Teams

Since there is growing evidence that adults learn a great deal through informal interactions during inservice education, one of the early tasks in a workshop should be to develop learning teams or groups. Time should be taken to allow participants to get acquainted, share perceptions of what they hope to learn, and identify objectives and/or activities that they will pursue together during the workshops.

The development of learning teams or groups is usually done through very informal means. Those who plan and conduct successful workshops for educators recommend structured experiences to build relationships and skills necessary to promote group learning. The Institute for the Development of Educational Activities (/I/D/E/A/) opens their clinical workshops on individualized instruction with a sequence of small group activities that enables participants to get to know each other, to clarify values about issues related to the workshop, to solve problems, and to trust and help each other learn. Davis and McCallon (1974) suggest that similar "warm up" activities be used when planning and conducting workshops.

These groups provide an excellent setting for teachers and administrators to share the new insights and learnings and solve problems encountered during the workshop. The research by Allen Tough (1967) in Canada and the Rapports (1975) in England suggests that this kind of informal learning is valued by adult learners. There also is evidence which shows small group learning promotes growth in higher order cognitive development (/I/D/E/A/, 1971).

Choices for Participants

It is critical to involve participants in selecting at least some objectives, activities, and materials they will use in an inservice workshop. This involvement responds directly to the adult learners' need for control over their own learning. It also enables the participants to select those things which they believe have the greatest potential for helping them improve their job performance and makes them responsible for their own professional growth. Finally, it facilitates the personalization and individualization of inservice.

At the most general level, participants might choose whether they will continue in a workshop after they have had an orientation to the objectives and activities. Once this choice is made, there may or may not be other choices available.

A good example of this approach is used in some workshops conducted by the Staff Development Center in the Ferguson-Florissant School District in St. Louis County, Missouri. Several weeks prior to the workshop the Center searches the computerized needs assessment data for those persons who reported a need to pursue the objectives of the upcoming workshop. The staff of the Center then mails an invitation to teachers who might be interested in participating in a workshop. This invitation includes a description of the workshop with the time, objectives, activities, and other data that might help teachers decide whether this kind of training fits their professional growth needs. Based upon this information, and, for some, additional discussions with Staff Development Center personnel, teachers decide whether they will participate.

At the same time the teachers receive this invitation, their principals also are informed that one of their teachers has received notification of a workshop. This enables the principal to encourage teachers or other staff to participate in inservice that relates to the school's goals for improvement. It also alerts the principals to inservice activities in which they may wish to participate so they can be supportive of their teachers during both the training and on-the-job follow-up activities. Principals are key people in school improvement and change; their encouragement of staff to participate in workshops, involvement in inservice with teachers, and assistance to teachers in follow up after training increase significantly the chances of real, lasting change in professional performance among the faculty (Berman and McLaughlin, 1978).

Choices should also be provided within a workshop. Participants should have options concerning what learning activities they pursue. Some learn best through reading, others through viewing and listening, others through talking with people who have done what they are trying to learn, and still others by observing and then asking questions about the how and why of a particular practice. Since this is the case and we lack precise measures to assess learning style or preference, our best recourse is to provide for all of these options in a workshop's learning experiences. The participants can then select the options they believe fit their style. Of course, the workshop leader may guide or require objectives and activities when they are appropriate and essential.

The /I/D/E/A/ clinical workshop used by educators to introduce Individually Guided Education provides options for learning. This workshop is structured so that participants may choose to learn about different approaches to individualizing instruction through reading print materials, viewing filmstrips, or getting information from the workshop leader. They also may learn by themselves or in groups. The choices for learning experiences were planned into the workshop design. The print and audiovisual materials were selected and developed to promote student choice in learning. Participants can also select objectives other than those that are required. Thus, this workshop provides participants considerable control over the objectives and activities of their professional development.

Experiential Learning

Another essential feature of effective inservice education is the opportunity to participate in simulations or experience-based learning (Wood and Thompson, 1980). Experiential learning begins with an examination of different examples of the intended learning. Participants then implement one or more examples of the principles, skills, or other learnings in structured or laboratory situations. Following each activity, the learners discuss their experience in small groups and develop generalizations from their learning. After several such experiences and discussions, the participants have developed their own concepts and a set of generalizations that may be applied in real work settings. Experiential learning or learning-by-doing is a recurring cycle in input, experience, analysis, generalization, and application. It is similar to many scientific processes and is founded upon well established learning theory and research (Kolb and Fry, 1975).

There is considerable support for employing experiential learning as part of inservice training. According to James Coleman (1976), what is learned through this process: (1) is not tied to abstract words but to real experiences that can be drawn upon when one is back in the work setting, (2) is remembered over a longer period of time, and (3) is more likely to be used after the training is completed. Research by Joyce and Peck (1977) shows that teachers and administrators believe that this type of activity ought to be included in the plan of an inservice workshop.

Another advantage of learning by doing is that it helps the participants develop a gestalt of the changes in behavior and programs to be implemented. It is important for those who are trying to change their professional behaviors to conceptualize the entire change. Too often inservice education occurs in bits and pieces and teachers and administrators do not understand how what they are learning fits together. Understanding the whole gives meaning to learning the parts, that is, the variety of skills, strategies, content, and attitudes essential for implementation of a change in practice.

Experiential learning activities also enable educators to see how the things they are learning can operate "back home." Teachers and administrators like other adult learners, are willing to learn something that they perceive will be useful to them back in the "real world." Inservice experiences in a work setting very much like their own help them understand how their new learning might assist them to be more efficient on the job. They also enable the participants to see how new behaviors and programs can operate in the context of a school setting.

To make these practicum experiences as real as possible for the participants, the setting for training should be similar to the one in which the participants usually work. The more the teachers see the students, school facilities, instructional materials, and equipment used in the training as similar to their own situation, the more likely they are to view the experiential activities and what is to be learned as real and applicable to them. Even if the training does not include direct experience with students, inservice should occur in a school or work setting similar to those typical for the participants.

There are a number of successful programs that can serve as examples for planning experiential inservice programs. One of these, the Professional Development and Program Improvement Center (PDPIC) of the Long Beach Unified School District in California, has been described by Wood and Thompson (1980) :

The Long Beach PDPIC was organized in 1969 as part of a statewide network of professional development centers in California. These centers were intended to strengthen instructional techniques in reading and mathematics. In the Long Beach center, this has been accomplished through a staff development program with four major components: (1) teaching reading and/or mathematics objectives, (2) diagnostic and prescriptive instructional skills, (3) clinical supervision, and (4) follow-up, maintenance, and refinement. Training in each component closely follows the steps of experiential learning.

Participants initially receive an overview of the entire training sequence in all components. The first skill in component one is then introduced and demonstrated by the workshop facilitators. After a short time for preparation, the participants practice the skill with small groups of five to ten students in local school classrooms. Each participant is observed by one or more of the other participants while teaching the practice lesson. After the practice sessions, each instructor and observer group meets to analyze the lesson. This cycle of overview, model, practice, and analysis is repeated for all of the skills in each training component. The entire inservice training process lasts about three to six weeks.

During the workshop, participants are released from classroom responsibilities by a special team of master substitutes who have already been trained in the skills considered in the workshop. Participants work in small groups to promote learning from each other. The team members provide one another with feedback about their performance as they attempt to practice the behaviors set in the objectives and criteria of this experience-based inservice program. Participants also have access to demonstration classrooms where the skills being learned can be observed and to print and audiovisual materials to supplement their training and provide alternative learning experiences. The entire workshop is conducted within a local school (pp. 377-378) .

The /I/D/E/A/ clinical workshop on individualizing instruction is another excellent example of an experiential workshop. Over the past seven years, it has been used to train approximately 17,000 teachers and administrators in elementary, junior high, and high schools throughout the United States. In the workshop, the participants teach students in an actual school setting. The participants work as members of a teaching team, instruct multi-aged classes, use a systematic diagnostic approach to planning and teaching, help students develop responsibility for planning and assessing their own learning, serve as teacher-counselors to students, design and conduct their own inservice, clarify their values related to teaching and learning, and help their teammates improve their instruction through peer observation.

This 10-to-12-day workshop follows a learning sequence of experiences—analysis—understanding—planning—application. It allows participants to try out their new learnings in a real school where the threat of failure is limited. The results of a study of the /I/D/E/A/ clinical workshop by Wood and Neill (1976) indicate that this clinical approach to inservice education holds considerable promise for helping change commitment and classroom practice in the area of individualization.

Leadership

The success of any workshop rests heavily on the leadership provided by the people who direct the inservice learning experience. Who should lead inservice training? How much structure and support should be provided participants as they move through their training and are given increasing responsibility for their own inservice activities? What should the director of inservice do to promote learning? Are there particular things the workshop leader should do at certain times during training? Each of these questions is important to consider when examining leadership in the Training Stage.

The selection of leadership for a workshop should be based upon expertise, not position. Whenever possible, local personnel, preferably peers of those to be trained, should direct inservice training. Successful implementation and continuation of changes in school practice appear to be more likely when inservice is conducted by local staff (Berman and McLaughlin, 1978). While using local teachers and administrators as directors of a workshop may be preferred by educators and reduce the threat of negative judgments by one's supervisor during training, it does not replace the primary criterion of expertise.

The workshop leaders should have indepth knowledge about what is to be learned. They also need to be skilled in planning and conducting inservice for professionals, particularly in the areas being considered in the workshop they will direct. The leader should be someone who has already achieved the content, skills, and attitudinal objectives to be learned by the participants.

When local leadership is not available, outside consultants can be employed. A more efficient and appropriate means, however, of getting local leadership is to train a cadre of district teachers and administrators to direct inservice activities. The training of local staff reduces the problems of high cost and limited availability of outside consultants. Through this strategy, key district and school personnel can be prepared by local or outside experts to conduct training sessions for their peers.

There are a number of effective inservice programs that start with the training of local personnel to conduct local inservice. The Institute for the Development of Educational Activities, for example, trains district staff to conduct clinical workshops on individualization in their local schools. The training consists of participating in a clinical workshop; discussing the what and why of the workshop activities; and planning and conducting clinical workshops for their own teachers and administrators.

Another example of how to train local personnel is being employed by the Jersey Shore School District, a small district with limited funds in rural Pennsylvania. During the initial stages of an inservice program, this district contracted with consultants from Penn State University to help the local administrators and teachers design an individualized approach to teaching mathematics and to train four master teachers. The master teachers in turn trained all the fourth-grade teachers to use this mathematics program. The next year the fourth-grade teachers and the four master teachers trained the fifth-grade teachers. The third year the fifth-grade teachers and the master teachers trained the sixth-grade teachers. The training included the involvement of the participant as a full teaching partner in the classrooms of the trainer who was using the individualized approach to math.

The Lincoln Public Schools in Nebraska have also prepared teachers, counselors, and other personnel to conduct workshops for the staff. Each year the Director of Staff Development and other administrators identify staff members who have developed expertise through district inservice and could conduct training programs related to school and district priorities. These teachers then become inservice leaders for the district and receive some released-time, leadership stipends, and special recognition to compensate them for providing inservice to their colleagues in the district.

A second area of inservice leadership that needs to be considered is the extent to which workshop directors focus their attention on giving directions and giving socioemotional support to participants. Hersey and Blanchard (1977), in their discussion of what they call situational leadership, suggest that the amount of direction and socioemotional support provided workshop participants by leaders should vary depending upon the extent to which participants have mastered the inservice objectives. Situational leadership suggests that as inservice participants progress from having none of the distinct knowledge and skills to full understanding, ability, and willingness to perform the tasks defined by the workshop objectives, the amount of structure and reinforcement provided should be managed and adjusted systematically.

For those teachers and administrators in a workshop who have little or no competence in the areas of desired learning, the leader should stress giving direction and de-emphasize reinforcement-relationship behaviors. In this situation, the director structures activities to provide information or resources that participants must use to learn the what, how, when, and where of the tasks being taught in the workshop. De-emphasizing reinforcement-relationship behavior does not mean the leader is unfriendly, just that more time is spent directing participants on what and how to do or behave. As the teachers and administrators in the training session begin to demonstrate the ability to handle the professional behaviors presented, the leader needs to reduce directing behavior moderately and to increase socioemotional support in the form of positive feedback and reinforcement. It is during this time that the leader identifies those things the learners are doing correctly and redirects them to specific changes they need to make in their performance. Once the objectives are achieved and being practiced by the participants during the experiential component of the workshop, the leader moves to low directing behaviors and extensive use of positive reinforcement. As soon as the leader perceives that participants no longer need either directing or socioemotional support, they should let the participants operate on their own.

Thus, as participants go through a workshop, the director's behavior will typically move from high direction and low socioemotional support, to high direction and high socioemotional support, to low direction and high socioemotional support, and finally to low direction and low socioemotional support. This sequence enables the participant to become more and more independent of the workshop leadership. It also requires that the inservice director constantly observe and be available to participants during a workshop. The directors must see their job as one of responding to participants' needs and moving them toward independence.*

Providing Feedback

As the director guides the activities of the workshop, there is a need to provide early opportunities for successful experience. Immediate failure, especially when the participants are risking a substantial change in their current practice, should be avoided. This suggests that the director needs to spend time early in the workshop observing to make sure participants are getting the kind of assistance they need to be successful. It also means that some procedure should be provided for participants to share their frustration and concerns.

This kind of feedback can be obtained through informal conversations between the directors and the participants at the end of each day. Each participant can also be asked to use 3 x 5 cards on a regular basis to report their feelings, problems, and new insights to the workshop director. Another means of getting feedback is to plan periodic sessions where the director can listen to the learning teams discuss what they are learning, their successes, and their problems. The need for participants to share learning and to help each other solve problems is essential regardless of whether the director uses these meetings to diagnose progress and problems.

Teachers and administrators both believe that they learn a great deal from such open-ended feedback sharing sessions (Joyce and Peck, 1977). In fact, this type of interaction is essential for workshop participants to see the wide applications of the concept and procedure being considered during training. Such meetings also provide peer support and encouragement needed by those having problems.

Commitment to Implement

At the close of the workshop, the participants need to review what they've learned with the workshop leaders and their learning team. Participants should also devise a tentative plan for implementing what has been learned into their daily activities back on the job before they leave a workshop. This plan should include goals, a timeline, procedures, and assistance needed to institutionalize their new professional behaviors and

* More information about situational leadership and instruments to measure which leadership styles are appropriate for particular groups or individuals are available from the Learning Resources Corporation in LaJolla, California.

knowledge. The details of what might be included in this plan are presented in the discussion of the next stage of inservice.

The plan represents a commitment to use what has been learned. It also provides those responsible for staff development with specific information about the kind of assistance that will be needed to assure that the results of the inservice will be put into practice.

Evaluation

The evaluation data collected in the Training Stage are both formative and summative. Throughout the training, formative data are collected to determine workshop participants' progress toward objectives, the effectiveness of the learning experience, and the needed changes in the inservice activities. Data are also collected to determine the overall effects of the workshop on participants and the extent to which the inservice plan was actively implemented. The summative data should include measures of cognitive, behavioral, and attitudinal change in the participants related to the objectives of the workshop. Opportunity for participants to report unanticipated learnings should also be provided—sometimes these are the most important results of the training (Wood and Neill, 1976).

Stage IV: Implementation

On-the-job implementation of what has been learned in the Training Stage should begin as soon as possible. A common complaint about inservice programs is that what is learned seldom finds its way into practice. This may be due to the lack of attention given to providing follow-up assistance to educators as they attempt to use what they have learned in inservice in their classroom or administrative work.

The Implementation Stage deals with making sure what is learned in inservice training becomes part of the activity and behavior of educators in the work setting. The thrust is to provide an environment that will support the transition of inservice learnings from the workshop setting into the daily activities of classroom teaching or administrative operations. A supportive environment includes on-call assistance from peers and administrators, formal and informal recognition and approval by immediate superiors, and availability of funds, time, and other resources to support post-training adaptation and implementation in work "back home."

When participants leave a workshop, they should have a written plan for implementing their learning. This plan should be shared with

the principal or other appropriate administrators so they can help monitor and support those plans. The shorter the time between the training
and action the more likely the momentum developed during the inservice will remain a positive force, the more likely what was learned
will be remembered, and the less likely the participants will return to
their old ways of operating.

Follow-Up Assistance

A great deal of assistance is frequently needed when educators first
attempt to use, on the job, what they have learned in the controlled
environment of an inservice workshop. For example, as teachers begin
to use new materials and teaching strategies, they may find they need to
modify what they have learned to fit their particular situations. They
need ideas and encouragement from their peers and supervisory personnel to adapt and implement what they have used and done successfully in inservice training.

On-call help can be provided by both peers and administrators, but
those providing assistance must know enough to be helpful. It is important
to make sure that such expertise is immediately available during Implementation.

One way to ensure this assistance is to have a team of teachers from
a school go through a workshop. After the training, this cadre of school
staff can call upon each other as they need assistance. The principal of
the school might also go through the workshop either with the teachers
or with other principals. This prepares him or her to serve as a resource
to teachers who are making changes in their instructional practices. A
third option might be to assign district supervisory staff to help teachers
in a school on an on-call basis. The supervisors would stimulate and
respond to requests for help.

When possible, the decisions about the who, what, and how of
assistance should be controlled by the persons requesting it. There are
several means by which school personnel can be made more comfortable
about requesting help. One is to have groups of teachers or administrators
who were in the same learning team during training meet periodically
with inservice personnel to discuss how they are implementing their
plans to use their learnings from their workshop.

This team would operate as a problem solving, sharing, self-help
group. They might observe and provide feedback to each other about
the strengths and alternatives related to how each of them is making use
of the professional strategies and skills they learned. Of course, it helps

if regular meetings and peer observations are included in the plans developed at the end of the Training Stage *prior* to returning to their classroom or office.

Another means of encouraging requests for help is through follow-up meetings between the workshop directors and participants. These sessions include discussions of what the participants have done to implement new strategies in the classroom, their problems and questions, and direct observation in the work setting by the workshop leader. All these activities provide the teacher or administrator with a chance to request help from an "expert."

Jersey Shore School District in Pennsylvania, discussed earlier, uses this type of follow-up to help teachers learn to individualize elementary mathematics. About two or three weeks after inservice training is completed, the trainers visit the teachers they trained. Since the teachers return to classrooms that have been reorganized with the materials, equipment, and record-keeping procedures used in the workshop, post-training visits provide opportunities to discuss things that are working well and things that are not. They also provide the inservice directors with a chance to observe the teachers they trained and provide feedback on how things are going. The results of such visits are helpful suggestions about how to improve teaching strategies, use teacher aides, and plan for additional inservice.

The use of clinical supervision by peers or administrators provides an excellent opportunity for educators to request assistance in implementing the things they have learned into their daily work behaviors. In this supervisory process, the persons to be observed control what they want observed and what they want to improve in their current practice. Once the contract is set for the observation—usually related to a specific outcome the person to be observed wishes to implement—two or three faculty members, who understand what the observee is trying to do, plan and complete the observation. They limit their data collection, analysis, and feedback to those questions or areas identified by the person observed. This observation team reports the objective data they recorded related to the areas of improvement selected by the observee and they discuss alternative ways to implement the outcomes to which they were asked to respond (Goldhammer, 1969). This approach to assisting teachers install new knowledge and skills into their instructional strategies has been used by many elementary and secondary schools in the United States (Withall and Wood, 1979; Wood and Neill, 1976).

Administrative Support and Recognition

Even with adequate help to implement inservice learnings into on-going school programs, lasting change in practices is unlikely unless the principal and other administrators legitimize these changes. They can do this (1) through giving formal and informal recognition to people who are making the desired changes and (2) through budgeting funds and other resources to support specific changes in practice.

Recognition can take many forms. Informal contacts between central office personnel, principals, and teachers can be used to encourage and reinforce the importance of the changes that are being made by staff members. Faculty meetings can be a forum to recognize efforts to change professional practices. Having peers visit those applying new strategies to observe or discuss changes is another informal way of reinforcing improved professional practices. Central office personnel visiting the school to discuss new practices or visiting teachers' classes also communicate that efforts to improve performance are valued.

More formal means of giving recognition to those who are putting inservice learnings into action include such things as (1) newspaper releases about changes that have and are being made, (2) reports in district or school newsletter and announcements about specific faculty or groups of faculty who are making important changes, (3) access to additional professional travel funds, (4) opportunities to participate as inservice leaders for other educators, and (5) provisions for released-time to work out problems related to implementing or extending changes being made in practice. Somehow, some way, administrators, especially the principal, must communicate in either their informal or formal actions that the efforts to implement the learnings of inservice are important.

The district budget should also reflect administrative commitment to change. Funds must be available to pay for instructional materials, released-time for staff, and follow-up support personnel to implement inservice outcomes. Care must be taken in the Planning Stage or even earlier to make sure that funds necessary for improvement programs will be available in the Implementation Stage. It also is essential that those trying to implement new practices in Stage IV know the limits of the resources available.

Leadership

Leadership in this stage is provided by those most competent to assist educators incorporate their inservice learning into their daily activities. As in the Training Stage, peer assistance and shared leadership should be given priority. The principal, however, must give support and encouragement, and help in getting the assistance and resources needed to implement changes in the staff's professional behaviors.

Whoever guides the activities in the Implementation Stage must again consider the balance between directing and socioemotional support behaviors of situational leadership. In most cases, those responsible for implementation on the job will give high emotional support and use some directing behaviors. As skills and confidence increase, assistance and support should be systematically withdrawn.

Evaluation Data

Evaluation data collected at this point in the inservice cycle provide information about the extent to which what has been learned in the inservice training has become part of daily practice. Just prior to this stage, baseline data on students are collected. As desired practices increase and are recorded in the work setting, corresponding data should be collected to determine their effect on students.

Stage V: Maintenance

New professional behaviors are not permanent even when they have become part of the ongoing activities of a school. The Maintenance Stage of inservice programs establishes continuous monitoring to determine whether new behaviors are still being practiced and goals met.

Monitoring can be done in several ways. Self-monitoring can be done using video- and audiotape recordings of classroom activities that can be played back by a teacher to help examine his or her own behavior. Student feedback can be obtained by using interviews or questionnaires that focus on a topic of interest to teachers who want to monitor their own behavior. Peer supervision is another effective technique that can be used. Teachers can be trained to use clinical techniques to observe in each other's classrooms and provide objective data as feedback (Withall and Wood, 1979). Teacher interviews and questionnaires are also tools for monitoring continued use of content, skills, and strategies implemented in Stage IV (Halvorsen and Paden, 1976; Jones, 1973).

In the Maintenance Stage the key is continuous review as part of the regular supervisory process used in schools. A school staff must remain focused on the professional behaviors that are supposed to be operating in their school and committed to the continued improvement and refinement of these behaviors.

This stage of inservice programs completes the cycle by generating new data and needs that can be used to plan additional staff development activities and to begin the five stages again. Summative data are also collected to determine the effects of the changes by teachers on students' achievement or by administrators on those with whom they work.

Coordinating Inservice Programs

Up to this point, we have discussed the five stages in designing staff development programs primarily as they apply to a single school or school staff. While the school is the principal unit of change (Goodlad, 1975), staff development programs exist in the larger context of school district goals and state and federal guidelines. Also, as we pointed out in earlier chapters, universities, regional service centers, and state departments offer extensive resources for inservice training. In such a pluralistic environment, inservice programs and resources must be coordinated in some way.

Professional development begins within the individual school. Faculty and administrators work and grow within the ecology or culture of their own building. At the building level, staff development can involve a group of staff members who participate in planning professional development programs. This group can coordinate existing inservice programs with the demands for training that special projects and urgent programs impose. As the principal gatekeepers for staff development programs at the school level, the members of such a group can integrate information from outside the school within the five stages of designing inservice programs. This can eliminate the all too common experience of many educators who must participate in training programs for many different purposes, each planned by a different group. Coordinating committees exist in many schools and are known as program improvement councils, professional growth advisory committees, or instructional improvement committees.

In a larger context, inservice programs may be coordinated among schools that are organized in clusters or leagues. Such networks may be based upon shared goals, feeder systems, geography, or some other common criteria. Again it is committees that coordinate programs among schools. The cluster committee may be composed of representatives from each participating school, school district central administration, neighboring colleges and universities, and local service agencies. A typical cluster or league includes five to ten schools. The advantages of a cluster system include the more efficient use of resources, more effective dissemination of solutions to common problems, and the widespread support of professional growth practices. While the most important focus for staff development is the single school, leagues can support individual schools by making effective use of resources. Examples of this kind of system are found in the regional networks of the Teacher Corps program (Goddu, 1978) and in the League of Cooperating Schools (Goodlad, 1975).

The Question of Time

Another important issue is that of time. The guidelines described here are in sharp contrast to many past efforts in staff development in that they describe a long-range growth cycle of four or five years' duration. The experience of federally-funded programs in the last decade has led to revised time expectations for such programs as Teacher Corps, which recently changed its format from a two-year to a five-year funding cycle.

Professional growth is a complex, human task. It requires a climate conducive to learning and change. It is based upon clear goals and objectives derived from careful needs assessment. It is promoted by the effective use of diverse resources. It includes opportunities for field-testing, feedback, and adjustment. All these things take time to achieve.

We have described here the tasks and considerations necessary to plan and conduct effective staff development programs. This approach is a tool that can help in designing inservice education activities. It is important to remember, however, that the five stages described are not necessarily discrete, sequential steps; there is overlap in the application of these stages. Training, Implementation, and Maintenance may occur simultaneously within an inservice program as individuals and small groups progress at different rates in their pursuit of the same inservice outcomes. Also, there is a persistent need to review commitments periodically, to maintain facilitative climates, and to revise plans for training. This underscores the importance of viewing inservice education as a continuous, professional activity.

Throughout the five stages we have described, certain principles emerge that appear to be key considerations in the design of inservice education activities. The following list is intended to summarize these considerations, the critical characteristics of effective professional development programs.

Critical Characteristics of Professional Development Programs

■ Inservice education should be conducted in a supportive climate of trust, peer support, open communication, and staff commitment to a set of clearly understood norms for functioning in an institution (clear roles, program definition, instruction procedures, goals).

■ Inservice education goals should be based upon a common set of expectations held by the participants for normative behaviors that are essential to performing their professional roles in their institution.

■ Successful inservice education requires support from administration and school boards including time, personnel, training materials, and funds to enable the training necessary to implement educational programs in their school district.

■ Decisions concerning the objectives, experiences, and assessment of inservice education should be cooperatively developed by those involved in and affected by the training program.

■ Inservice education should be based upon assessed needs of participants. A need is defined as a gap between the expected professional performance and actual performance in the work setting.

■ Inservice education should model the instructional behaviors desired of participants.

■ Inservice education programs should be demanding and set high but reasonable standards of performance for participants.

■ Inservice education programs should have three major components: (1) attitude, (2) pedagogical skills, and (3) substantive knowledge.

■ Inservice education should prepare educators to implement research findings and best practice related to carrying out their job responsibilities.

■ Inservice education should be decentralized; focus on actual school problems, goals, needs, and plans; and be conducted, whenever feasible, in the school setting.

■ Inservice education should emphasize use of rewards (such as opportunity, increased antonomy, participation in decision making, increased competence, success, and advancement) which have been shown to promote high commitment and performance.

■ Inservice education should be based upon clear, well understood, specific goals and objectives that are congruent with institutional and personal goals.

■ Inservice education should provide options for participants that will accommodate individual professional needs and learning styles (timing, sequence, pace, interests, goals, delivery systems).

■ Inservice education should be experientially based with opportunities to select, adapt, and try out new professional behaviors in real and simulated work settings.

■ Central office personnel and school administrators should support inservice education through their participation in training activities with their peers and subordinates.

■ Inservice education programs should provide for follow-up and "on call" assistance to educators as they use their new skills and understandings in the work setting after they have been trained.

■ Leadership in inservice education programs should be situational and emphasize authority by competence and expertise rather than by position.

■ Evaluation of inservice education should be both formative and summative and should examine the immediate effect on participants, extent of transfer to the work setting, and the effect on achieving institutional goals.

REFERENCES

Berman, Paul, and McLaughlin, Milbrey W. *Federal Programs Supporting Educational Change, Vol. VIII: Implementing and Sustaining Innovations.* Santa Monica, Calif.: Rand, 1978.

Blumberg, Arthur. "OD's Future in Schools—Or Is There One?" *Education and Urban Society* 8 (February 1976) : 213-226.

Burton, G. E.; Pathak, D. S.; and Burton, D. B. "The Gordon Effect in Nominal Grouping." *University of Michigan Business Review* 30 (July 1978).

Coleman, James S. "Differences Between Experiential and Classroom Learning." In *Experiential Learning: Rationale, Characteristics, and Assessments*, pp. 49-61. Edited by Morris T. Keeton and associates. Washington, D.C.: Jossey-Bass 1976.

Davis, Larry Nolan, and McCallon, Earl. *Planning, Conducting, and Evaluating Workshops.* Austin, Tex.: Learning Concepts, 1974.

Edelfelt, Roy A. "The Shifting Emphasis to Inservice Teacher Education." In *Inservice Education: Criteria for and Examples of Local Programs*, pp. 3-8. Edited by Roy A. Edelfelt. Bellingham: Western Washington State College, 1977.

Ernst, William. "What Makes a Workshop Jell?" *Educational Leadership* 31 (March 1974) : 496-498.

Ford, David L. "Nominal Group Technique: An Applied Group Problem Solving Activity." In *The 1975 Annual Handbook for Group Facilitators*. Edited by John Jones and William Pfeiffer. LaJolla, Calif.: University Associates, 1975.

Goddu, Roland. "Techniques and Strategies for Demonstrating Effective Practices in Inservice Teacher Education Programs." *Inservice Education: Demonstrating Local Programs*, p. 33. Edited by Roy A. Edelfelt. Bellingham: Western Washington State College, 1978.

Goldhammer, Robert. *Clinical Supervision and Special Methods for the Supervision of Teachers.* New York: Holt, Rinehart, and Winston, 1969.

Goodlad, John. *Dynamics of Educational Change.* New York: McGraw-Hill, 1975.

Halvorsen, James, and Paden, Jon S. *User's Guide for Survey of Effective School Practices.* Dayton, Ohio: Institute for the Development of Educational Activities, Inc., 1976.

Hart, Helen A. "Self-Renewal: A Model." *Educational Leadership* 31 (March 1974) : 499-501.

Hersey, Paul, and Blanchard, Kenneth H. *Management of Organizational Behavior: Utilizing Human Resources,* 3rd ed. Englewood Cliffs, N.J.: Prentice-Hall, 1977.

Institute for the Development of Educational Activities. *Learning in the Small Group*. Dayton, Ohio: Institute for the Development of Educational Activities, 1971.

Jones, John E. "The Sensing Interview." In *The 1973 Handbook for Group Facilitators*. Edited by William Pfeiffer and John Jones. LaJolla, Calif.: University Associates, 1973.

Joyce, Bruce, and Peck, Lucy. *Inservice Teacher Education Report 11: Interviews*. Syracuse, N.Y.: National Dissemination Center, Syracuse University, 1977.

Kolb, D. A., and Fry, R. "Toward an Applied Theory of Experiential Learning." In *Theories of Group Processes*. Edited by Carl L. Cooper. New York: John Wiley, 1975.

McLaughlin, Milbrey, and Berman, Paul. "Retooling Staff Development in a Period of Retrenchment." *Educational Leadership* 35 (December 1977) : 191-192.

Rapport R., and Rapport, R. N. *Leisure and the Family Life Cycle*. London: Routledge and Kegan Paul, 1975.

Rubin, Louis J. "The Case for Staff Development." In *Professional Supervision for Professional Teachers*, pp. 34-38. Edited by Thomas J. Sergiovanni. Alexandria, Va.: Association for Supervision and Curriculum Development, 1975.

Tough, Allen. *Learning Without a Teacher*. Toronto: Ontario Institute for Studies in Education, 1967.

Tough, Allen. *A Study of the Major Reasons for Beginning and Continuing a Learning Project*. Toronto: Ontario Institute for Studies in Education, 1968.

VandeVen, A., and Delbecq, A. "The Effectiveness of Nominal, Delphi, and Interacting Group Decision-making Processes." *Academy of Management Journal* 17,4 (1974) : 605-621.

Wagstaff, Lonnie, and McCullough, Tom. "Inservice Educators: Education's Disaster Area." *Administrator's Notebook* 21 (May 1973) .

Withall, John, and Wood, Fred H. "Taking the Threat Out of Classroom Observation and Feedback." *Journal of Teacher Education* 30 (January-February 1979) : 55-58.

Wood, Fred H., and Thompson, Steven R. "Guidelines for Better Staff Development." *Educational Leadership* 37 (February 1980) : 374-378.

Wood, Fred H., and Neill, John F. *A Study of the Effects of the /I/D/E/A/ Clinical Workshop: Report Two*. Dayton, Ohio: Charles F. Kettering Foundation, 1976.

5

Evaluating Staff Development
Daniel L. Duke and Lyn Corno

THE EVALUATION COMPONENT needs to provide information about:

1. The overall condition of the staff development system (the environment created to facilitate professional growth).

2. The adequacy of the processes being used to generate, govern, and maintain the system.

3. The effects of specific training thrusts on participants, the school, and children.

4. Side effects, both positive and negative, on participants and on the organization.

Daniel Duke and Lyn Corno have summarized basic evaluation theory and applied it to staff development. They deal with a wide range of areas, from political decisions (who, how, and why evaluation will be conducted, to whom and how results will be communicated), to assumptions and procedures for generating evaluations. They include a comprehensive example and criteria for evaluating the evaluation.

STAFF DEVELOPMENT EVALUATION, like staff development, is a basic organizational process. Sometimes it occurs on a formal basis; sometimes it takes place informally. No matter how it happens, staff development evaluation can have important consequences for organizations and their ability to achieve intended outcomes.

In this chapter we shall focus on formal staff development evaluation in schools. Our commitment is to make evaluation as unbiased and systematic as possible. Our hope is that educators who read this chapter will be able to plan and conduct their own staff development evaluations and to provide justification for their actions.

We regard the planning of a staff development evaluation as a decision-making process. Decisions must be made concerning: (1) evaluation design, (2) data collection, (3) methods of analysis, and (4) presentation of results. Besides these *technical decisions,* there are a variety of *political decisions* to be made: (1) the purposes of the evaluation, (2) the specific outcomes to be evaluated, (3) who is to be involved in carrying out the evaluation, (4) who will have access to the results, and (5) what resources are available for conducting the evaluation.

I. Our Approach and Assumptions

Staff development evaluations are similar to general program evaluations. Program evaluations may be as broad as a national assessment of proficiency testing or as specific as a measure of the effectiveness of computer-based instruction in one classroom. In either case the same basic decisions must be faced. Many references describe the nature and function of general program evaluations (see, for example, Weiss, 1972; Cronbach, 1978; and Cooley and Lohnes, 1976). Fewer resources focus specifically on staff development evaluations (Griffin, 1978, is an exception).

Viewing staff development evaluations as similar to general program evaluations entails at least five assumptions, all of which have been discussed by the authors of Chapter 4. We briefly reiterate these basic assumptions before describing the elements of a general program evaluation. First, we accept the notion that the school is the basic unit of change. Though a program may be applied to only a sample of individual teachers in a school, the general school climate nonetheless may be affected. Second, we believe local school districts have primary responsibility for staff development programs. While program needs may be determined by federal and state legislation, local school personnel are typically responsible for devising and implementing the programs. Third, the principal typically serves as "gatekeeper" for new programs in any school. It is often the principal's handling of staff development efforts that "makes the difference." Fourth, we concur that effective staff development programs are generated from some combination of thoughtful research and practice. Germs of ideas may result from research or from practice, but the most defensible efforts blend both endeavors. Finally, improvement in educational practice, as well as in evaluation of that practice, takes time and careful planning.

What exactly does a general program evaluation entail? We can turn to the prominent writers previously cited for answers. There are five critical elements of any program evaluation: goals, participants, program, setting, and outcomes (Weiss, 1972). Terminology varies slightly among various writers, but the basic elements are the same.

Goals, Questions, Objectives

The first task in any evaluation is to consider what is to be accomplished, given particular values. Put differently, the goals, questions, or objectives of the evaluation must be clarified. As our writers observe, the goals and questions to be clarified are the goals and questions of program users—school personnel, policy makers, funding agencies, and so on. Cronbach states "the evaluator's responsibility is to help others ask better questions and determine actions appropriate for their aims" (1978, p. 11a). Cooley and Lohnes add that "evaluation transcends research and extends into decision making" (1976, p. 3). Evaluators thus help users formulate and clarify goals and questions to the point where answers will aid decisions about future use of a program. Because evaluation extends into decision making, goals and questions are nearly always value-laden and political.

In the case of staff development evaluations, users may comprise all or part of a school community, including teachers, administrators, parents, students, and external participants, such as regional or state governments. Because the questions or goals formulated will likely affect these groups, it is important for various users to be consulted or involved in the planning of staff development evaluations. This point was emphasized in Chapter 4 as the authors discussed an effective approach to planning staff development. We will have more to say on how users may be involved in planning.

In any case, more questions will likely arise in evaluation plans than ultimately can be answered. To assist in giving priorities to evaluation questions, Cronbach recommends that more effort should be invested in evaluation when there are questions for which (a) relatively little is known about the answer and (b) decision makers care about the answer (1978, p. 441).

Participants, Units, Sample

In any program evaluation the program must be tried by some sample of participants. This sample may consist of individuals or groups, or some combination of both (schools are collections of individuals working in a group). In some evaluations, the individual is the unit of sampling. In others, the unit may be the school. In each case, however, the sample must usually be obtained from a population which consists of the range of participants available. Ideally, the units or participants selected for study are those *most like* the total range of participants available. The closer a sample resembles a population of interest, the more confidence we have that evaluation results will be true for the entire population.

Participants in staff development programs are most often teachers. They may also, however, be classroom aides, curriculum coordinators, or principals, depending on the program and its objectives. Random selection, or selecting participants so that all members of the population have an equal likelihood of being selected, is the method recommended for ensuring adequate sampling from a defined population. But random selection often is impossible in staff development evaluations. When units are teachers or principals, samples are typically smaller and voluntary. When sampling cannot be controlled, evaluators can still record how the sample was obtained, and carefully compare the sample to the population, attempting to show similarities and differences.

Programs, Treatment, Instructional Dimensions

If a program has not been implemented or used by participants, there is no point in evaluating it. An important part of any program evaluation, then, is determining the extent to which the program has been "realized" (Cronbach, 1978, p. 205). Weiss (1972) points out that programs, as well as goals, must be conceptualized, interpreted, and defined by evaluators (p. 43). It is conceivable that even the most structured programs may be realized differently than designers intend. Implementation may be incomplete (only a few sample teachers may actually participate) or modified (procedural changes may be made along the way); this is particularly the case during the "maintenance" stage of staff development. Recall from Chapter 4 the point that staff development implementation typically varies from program to program. It is suggested that such variations may depend on organizational factors, personality differences, and time-cost constraints. Two possible goals of staff development evaluation thus might be (a) to determine the extent to which a program was implemented and (b) to identify the factors that can maximize program implementation in future efforts. Documenting program implementation across situations should highlight similarities and differences and isolate the variables that seem to have the most influence on implementation. Cooley and Lohnes urge the use of continuous program evaluation rather than approaches that compare program users and non-users at one point in time.

Action Setting, Contextual Variables

Issues such as those mentioned above underscore the fact that no program can be implemented in isolation. Evaluations occur in a context or political arena. The setting influences the questions evaluators ask and the procedures they adopt as well as the outcomes they seek to assess (Fullan and Pomfret, 1977). No staff development evaluation is complete without some attempt to measure and analyze context variables.

In Chapter 4 we learned that staff development typically takes place in schools or school districts. These settings vary in a variety of ways, including such factors as organizational structure, explicit and implicit goals, communication patterns, and incentives for participating in staff development. In order to assess these and other context variables, evaluators are advised to use a diverse set of data gathering procedures. More will be said about data collection in the concluding sections of this chapter.

Outcomes

All of the previously mentioned factors—ranging from the intended goals of the program and the participants to the actual form of staff development and the context in which it occurs—are important, in large measure, because they have the potential to influence program outcomes. Therefore, the assessment of program outcomes is a most critical phase of staff development evaluation.

To ensure that accurate and meaningful outcome data are collected, evaluators need to consider the following: multiple measures, unanticipated outcomes, involvement of a wide range of participants, and the timing of data collection.

The use of multiple measures suggests that no one outcome indicator is sufficient to guide those who will use evaluation results. For each anticipated outcome, several measures, ranging perhaps from self-reports to non-participant observations, are desirable. Without multiple measures, it is impossible to assess the extent to which any single outcome indicator is measuring what it purports to measure.

Besides measuring anticipated outcomes, evaluators are advised to collect data on unanticipated outcomes as well. Duke (1978) has discussed the negative impact unanticipated outcomes can have on program success. Scriven (1972) urges the use of a goal-free evaluator—an individual who collects outcome data without prior knowledge of the intended outcomes of the program.

In collecting data on various program outcomes, evaluators need to involve a wide range of individuals participating in or affected by the program. In the case of staff development evaluation, these individuals might include teachers involved in the program, teachers electing not to participate, administrators and support staff, and students. Care must be taken to expose these people to the same basic questions. Tailoring data collection to particular role groups makes it difficult to compare or combine evaluation findings.

A final consideration when assessing program outcomes concerns the timing of data collection. In general, evaluations that obtain outcome data at one time only are less useful for decision-making purposes. Evaluators, when possible, should provide for outcome measures taken at several times during and after program implementation.

II. A Staff Development Evaluation with No Constraints

The discussion in the preceding section permits us to begin to imagine what a reasonably good staff development evaluation might look like. To refine this picture, we shall pretend for the moment that no practical constraints—such as money, time, personnel, or expertise—exist to impede our efforts. The value of the following evaluation design lies not in its implementability, but in its usefulness for thinking about ways to accommodate the constraints that inevitably surface to perplex evaluators. In other words, we make no pretense that constraint-free evaluations are ever possible in the real world.

Before outlining our model evaluation of staff development we must create a hypothetical program to evaluate. We present this program, hoping it incorporates at least some elements of staff development familiar to various consumers. We assume the program already has passed the "readiness" stage described in the chapter by Wood, Thompson, and Russell. Thus, participants are beginning to plan the staff development program and, with it, the evaluation design.

Project FITT. Faculty Interaction and Team Troubleshooting (FITT) is the title of an imaginary staff development program that seeks to reduce the seriousness of student behavior problems through early identification and intervention. Meeting twice a week with the principal and special consultants over the course of a semester, teachers learn how to diagnose the onset of learning or behavior problems and plan coordinated intervention strategies.

Project FITT places great emphasis on team troubleshooting, whereby all teachers at a given grade level meet together periodically to assess the progress of individual students. One assumption underlying the training program is that student behavior problems often result from poor coordination and communication among teachers. During bi-weekly afternoon workshops, teachers are expected to acquire skills in operating team troubleshooting sessions. In addition, teachers compile an inventory of resource people who may be called on for assistance in cases involving particularly troubled students. It is anticipated that one semester of workshops will permit the faculty of a given school to implement ongoing team troubleshooting, thereby reducing the number of serious student behavior problems and the level of teacher frustration.

Evaluation of Project FITT. To determine whether Project FITT should be instituted and maintained on a statewide basis, a comprehensive evaluation design was adopted. To facilitate our description of the evaluation design, we will ask a series of questions. Each question derives from our previous discussion of the elements of a program, and is linked to a specific decision point in the process by which the evaluation design is planned. These questions are purposely general enough to be used by anyone planning a program evaluation.

Decision 1. Who will be involved in planning the evaluation?

Representatives of all role groups potentially affected by Project FITT will be involved. This means that at least one administrator, board member, teacher, student, and parent will participate. Ultimate responsibility for the evaluation, however, should reside with a person or persons not directly involved in school activities. In the present case, two outside evaluation specialists will supervise the evaluation process. The specialists will be selected on the basis of their familiarity with districts such as the one under examination and their demonstrated capacity to produce informative evaluation reports.

Decision 2. What are the anticipated outcomes of Project FITT?

Project FITT is designed primarily to (a) reduce the frequency and severity of student behavior problems and (b) positively influence faculty attitudes toward their schools and teaching.

Decision 3. How will the anticipated outcomes be measured?

A. The primary outcome is the reduction of frequency and severity of student behavior problems. This will be measured in *several* ways:
   1. Disciplinary referrals to the office
      Disciplinary referrals to the office will require a written form on which information will be recorded on the alleged offense. Forms will be grouped on the basis of kind of misconduct. Weekly totals will be maintained.
   2. Unexcused absences
      Unexcused absences represent all absences not officially excused or accompanied by a verified excuse from a parent or guardian. Daily records of unexcused absences will be maintained.

3. Suspensions

   Suspensions constitute an official administrative action whereby a student is refused access to school for a designated time period. All suspensions, including the behavior problem leading to suspension, will be recorded.

4. Observations of student behavior

   Two observers will be trained to use an adaptation of a low-inference classroom observation system (Stallings, 1977, for example) designed to record student and teacher behavior as it occurs naturally. Observers will record data in each classroom on four different occasions. During these times, videotapes will also be made as a source of crossvalidation. In addition to these "low-inference data," observers will record any unusual incidents in detail.

5. Perceptions of student behavior

   Structured interviews will be held with administrators, teachers, students, and parents. Questions will deal with perceptions of the frequency and severity of student behavior problems for each student in each class.

B. The second major anticipated outcome is more positive faculty attitudes toward schools and teaching. Once again, multiple data sources will be used. The outcome will be measured by:

1. Teacher attitude interviews

   All teachers will participate in a one-hour structured interview designed to determine teacher satisfaction with their schools and their teaching. Selected items will be used from validated teacher attitude scales together with probing questions.

2. Teacher diaries

   All teachers will be paid to maintain daily diaries of their feelings toward work and problems they face at school.

Decision 4. How will unanticipated outcomes be measured?

By their nature, unanticipated outcomes cannot be specified in advance. However, it is possible to identify important aspects of the educational process that, though not directly addressed by Project FITT, might be affected in some way by it. These aspects include student grades and scores on standardized achievement tests, student rating of teacher effectiveness and subject matter relevance, and parent observations of student performance and interest in school. In addition to data on the preceding items, an ethnographic record of school life will be maintained by a resident observer.

Decision 5. Will any non-outcome data be collected?

Yes. To determine the extent to which Project FITT actually was implemented, a "running account" will be made of the workshops and related activities. In addition, workshop participants will be tested on their knowledge of the content of Project FITT and asked to assess the practical value of each component of the staff development program. These data will be of value in determining the project components that were particularly effective or ineffective and in assisting other groups interested in implementing the program.

Decision 6. Who will collect the data?

An evaluation team will be created, consisting of two evaluation specialists, a resident ethnographer, and various members of the school community. One evaluation specialist will be responsible for collecting data related to unanticipated outcomes. The other specialist will serve as a "goal-free evaluator" or an evaluator of unanticipated outcomes. Unlike the first specialist, the goal-free evaluator will not be apprised of the anticipated outcomes of the project. This provision permits the second specialist to collect data in an unbiased manner. The resident ethnographer will "live" in the school for the duration of the evaluation and maintain a running account of school activities, climate, and so on. To minimize the likelihood that valuable information will be withheld because it is collected by strangers, interviews will be conducted by local representatives of each role group. Thus, student leaders will be trained and paid to interview students. The same procedure will be followed for teachers and parents.

Decision 7. From whom will the data be collected?

Again, data will be gathered from all administrators, teachers, students, and parents.

Decision 8. When will the data be collected?

Data pertinent to anticipated and unanticipated outcomes will be collected during three phases—baseline (the semester prior to the beginning of Project FITT), immediate post-treatment (at the close of Project FITT), and follow-up (one year after the close of Project FITT). As indicated earlier, ethnographic data will be collected continuously during all three phases. During the semester-long series of bi-weekly workshops, additional data on the conduct of Project FITT also will be collected.

Decision 9. How can we be relatively certain that any observed differences were due to Project FITT (as opposed to some other factor or factors)?

Eight schools will be selected at random from a range of districts in the state. The schools will be matched as closely as possible on size of student body, size and attitudes of faculty, socioeconomic status of student body, and school location. From this group, four schools will be randomly designated experimental sites. Project FITT will be implemented in these schools. Arrangements will be made for alternative staff development activities to take place at the other four schools during this time period. These activities will have similar objectives, but no formal program will be provided. As a further mechanism for ensuring as close to controlled conditions as possible, students at each school will be randomly-assigned to classes in various subject matter areas. In this way, teachers cannot claim they had particularly difficult students. Data on anticipated outcomes, unanticipated outcomes, and non-outcome topics will be collected at each school. (Thus, four evaluation teams will be required.)

Decision 10. How will the data be analyzed?

All tallied data, including office referrals, absences, suspensions, classroom observations, direct questions, and achievement scores or other ratings obtained during interviews will be coded for computer keypunching. The computer setup also will contain codes for the three time periods of data collection and the evaluation design. Reliability statistics (indicating the extent to which data can be considered accurate) will be computed for student and teacher measurement scales (for example, achievement scores, teacher attitude scales) and classroom observations. Data will be analyzed descriptively with statistics such as arithmetic means, standard deviations, graphs and plots, correlations, and so on, at three levels of analysis: the school, the class, and the students. Inferential statistical tests will be made across levels, between treated and untreated groups, using all major outcomes. Data will be examined from multiple perspectives using variations on analysis of variance and generalized regression procedures. Qualitative data, including ethnographic field notes, teacher diaries, videotapes, and much of the interview information will not be quantified. Rather, an effort will be made to content analyze these data, looking for recurrent patterns or consistencies (see Holsti, 1969). The original form of the data will be maintained, with codings and group designations indicated for ease of interpretation.

Decision 11. How will the evaluation data be shared and used?

Evaluation data will be summarized in two written reports, one technical report containing all statistical results and conclusions, and one non-technical report using common language to discuss statistical findings. The technical report will be distributed to the ERIC system and condensed for journal publication. The non-technical report will be submitted to all participating administrators and teachers. Groups of 10 to 15 educators will then meet with the consultants for Project FITT and the evaluation specialists to review and discuss the evaluation and its implications. The evaluation results will serve also as the basis for plans to introduce Project FITT in the four non-experimental schools as a follow-up.

III. Making Evaluation Compromises in Light of Constraints

Recall that the preceding evaluation design decisions assumed no limitations in terms of time, personnel, expertise, or money. As a result, the design used multiple measures, eight schools matched on a number of important dimensions, a balanced experimental design, and random assignment of students to teachers. These controls helped increase the likelihood that the evaluation results would be valid and applicable to other schools in the state.

The real world of staff development evaluation, however, is subject to a variety of constraints. Small armies of data collectors equipped with videotape machines and sophisticated instruments typically are not available. Time often is limited. Persons affected by a new program may not be willing to cooperate with evaluators in all cases. What follows are some suggestions for how to conduct a reasonable evaluation given limitations on time, personnel, expertise, and resources. Once more we pose a series of questions that require decisions, but in this case they are compromise decisions.

Decision 1. What if insufficient funds exist to hire an experienced evaluation team?

Where expertise is limited, instrument development, scoring, and sophisticated data analysis must often give way to more anecdotal but careful recordkeeping. The decision rule: unless funds are available to train key persons and create a cadre of technical experts, extensive data collection is probably not advantageous.

The focus would be on critical incidents; teacher, student, parent interviews and diaries; and simple tallies of attendance and behavioral referrals, not on observations, test scores, or other numerical indices of performance. The experimental comparison would be replaced with an extensive examination of Project FITT in one or two schools.

The compromise just described leads to a kind of grass-roots effort, which, if done carefully and completely, can make an important contribution to the literature on staff development. A literature search revealed few such studies presently available (see Joyce and Showers, 1980, for example). Additionally, the absence of outside experts implies that Project FITT participants will serve as their own evaluators. While this casts doubt on the objectivity and generalizability of results, an "in-house evaluation" clearly can aid decision making *in the local context* (Snow, 1974).

Decision 2. What if the decision to evaluate is made after the commencement of the staff development program, thereby precluding the collection of baseline data?

In this instance, time is the problem. The evaluation decision was made too late to collect baseline data, so the proposed pre-mid-post design is impossible. As Campbell and Stanley (1966) pointed out, baseline information is not essential to good experimental design. This is particularly true if randomization remains possible. When schools, teachers, and students cannot be sampled and assigned randomly, initial group differences should at least be assessed and described. The major interest in a mid-post design where a comparison is possible (in the case of four or more schools) is the manner in which the "treated" and "untreated" groups diverge, and where they wind up after the treatment phase. Thus, the focus remains on both immediate and long range effects of the project.

Decision 3. What if it is impossible to conduct a follow-up evaluation one year after the end of the staff development project?

For whatever reasons, most published evaluations of staff development fail to report follow-up data. One answer when extensive follow-up is impossible is to carry out a minimal follow-up on a shorter time cycle. For example, classrooms can be observed one or two more times a month following the end of the project. School records concerning referrals and absences can be collected for two months instead of one year. Parents can be phoned two weeks after the project to check on such things as immediate reactions to changes in teacher behavior or feelings concerning any modifications in rewards implemented at the organizational level as a result of Project FITT. Still other outcomes can be examined that may have been mentioned in the model design, which would shed more light on immediate effects of staff development. Thus, a higher priority might be placed on data such as the "running account" of the workshops and related activities or teacher perceptions of the value of Project FITT.

Decision 4. What if the school climate is characterized by hostility toward evaluation?

The major concerns here are morale and accessibility to data. When evaluations are legislated and external agencies are commissioned to conduct the study, little may be done to protect the rights of participants. One result is that local support for the evaluation can diminish. We recommend drawing staff into the effort as planners and evaluators. Initially one or two persons usually can be counted on to exhibit the interest and enthusiasm necessary to undertake evaluation efforts. In particular, when "key opinion leaders" participate, the morale of the entire group may increase (Bem, 1970). As previously mentioned, the role of the principal is important in this regard.

As we said earlier, one of the best motivators for adults is to realize that their participation in a project or program will provide some payoff for relatively little effort. The key, then, is to determine the particular payoff that each participant values most (Cronbach, 1977). Such incentives will vary from person to person, so that while one teacher will become involved in return for a day or two of released time, another may do it simply for a chance to receive recognition as "an evaluator." To determine these incentives, there appears to be no substitute for consulting the persons involved on an individual basis. Getting the evaluation started with the assistance of a few interested teachers and administrators may well lead to more broad-based participation, which permits the sort of grass-roots approach discussed earlier. In any case, channeling hostility into productive energy requires, at the very least, careful planning and attention to the emotional needs of participants. As Cronbach and others (in press) have emphasized, evaluation is very much a political process.

Decision 5. What if it is impossible to collect data as planned, that is, using randomization procedures, from all teachers, students, and parents to the extent proposed?

Here the problem may be insufficient funds, personnel, time, the ethics of withholding treatment, or some combination of such possibilities. The point is that the proposed effort must, in some respects, be compromised. In this situation, it may be necessary to narrow the focus of the evaluation, concentrating only on key participants and critical aspects of the project, and measuring a well-defined set of outcomes, rather than taking a broad-lens view. Assuming that quality of information matters

more than quantity, and that situations defined as real are real in consequences (Thomas and Thomas, 1928, p. 572), we suggest an effort be
made to sample across schools within one key district, teachers within
schools, and students within classes. We also suggest collecting more subjective data. While a wide array of participants may not be available for
the staff development effort, data can be collected from a "representative"
subset of participants.

When randomization is impossible, the next best thing is to demonstrate that the sample chosen is typical of a particular population of
teachers, students, and parents. Descriptive data on personal characteristics, such as age, ability level, and socioeconomic status, are useful in
establishing that the sample is typical of a population. Also, rather than
collecting data that require on-site observation, videotaping, or extensive
record keeping, a limited number of personnel can be used to develop self-
scoring questionnaires that can be given to participants to complete.
During treatment and follow-up, teachers can be asked to maintain their
diaries as a major activity, rather than just the supporting activity proposed in the "model" evaluation. Participating administrators can do the
same. A project leader may be assigned the task of collecting and collating
teachers' written commentary.

Here the emphasis is on the process as much as the product, but the
process subjectively perceived across time and a typical group of participants. If the range of the study is limited, say, to one or two schools instead
of eight, an effort again can be made to show the extent to which the
two schools are similar or dissimilar to other schools in the state, and
how the project may be adapted to accommodate major school differences,
such as class size and socioeconomic status. School participants may not
only be asked to aid in scoring questionnaires and collecting diary data,
but also to assist in writing sections of the report. A team of teachers
working together to condense their anecdotal diary data into a meaningful
"Appendix" can stimulate productive professional introspection as well
as facilitate staff development evaluation.

IV. Evaluating Staff Development Evaluations

We have discussed the elements of program evaluations, presented a
model staff development evaluation, and identified ways the model
evaluation might be altered in light of practical constraints. In closing,
we think it appropriate to suggest some ways in which those called on to
design staff development evaluations might evaluate their efforts. To this
end we review and attempt to integrate three sets of criteria for evalua-

ting evaluations.* Griffin (1978) offers the only criteria specifically intended for staff development evaluation. The other two sets—one developed by Stufflebeam and others (1971) and critiqued by Guba (1975); the other offered by Guba, Ridings, and Stufflebeam (1979)—pertain in theory to any evaluation effort.

We have condensed these criteria into a series of basic questions evaluators might ask themselves. The questions encompass the following topics: comprehensiveness, technical quality, utility, and propriety. Our (constraint-free) model design in Section II takes all of these criteria into account. The discussion of compromises to the model design (Section III) is based on a relaxation of some of these criteria.

A. Comprehensiveness

1. Are data sufficient to address major questions?

Data are usually sufficient when measures are available on all participants and variables included in the evaluation goals or questions. When any aspect of a major evaluation is not addressed by the data (as when questions pertain to school effects and only teacher measures are available), data are insufficient.

2. Are data *rich* in information from multiple sources?

Availability of data does not always imply richness. When data provide *useful* information, they approximate the criterion of richness. Poor measures of important variables, or measures of unimportant variables, may provide little useful information. Similarly, an incompletely drawn description may be worse than no description at all.

3. Are data likely to yield *payoff* for investment of effort?

This is the traditional "cost effectiveness" question. Payoff here refers to the extent to which the questions are answered in a manner that will clarify choices for the decision maker. When data are so informative they point the way to a "better" alternative for a decision maker, payoff is higher (recall Cronbach's decision theory approach to effort). The worth of information must be weighed in conjunction with costs. So "effort" refers to human energy and financial investments as well. If the choice for a decision maker is whether or not to implement a staff development

---

* Our selection of schemes for evaluating staff development evaluation is not intended to suggest that other sets of criteria do not exist. For example, Michael Scriven's "Standards for the Evaluation of Educational Programs and Products" in Gary D. Borich, editor, *Evaluating Educational Programs and Products* (Englewood Cliffs, N.J.: Educational Technology Publications, 1974) is a very detailed scheme. We selected criteria from Griffin, Stufflebeam and others, and Guba, Ridings, and Stufflebeam because they seemed to cover the major issues facing evaluation planners with a minimum of technical terminology.

program districtwide, a well-documented set of information, suggesting "for some teachers, in some schools, but not districtwide," can be more informative than ambiguous data suggesting a general "yes." Moreover, the qualified decision would probably be less costly. A disorganized, vague set of information that suggests no clear-cut decision can be a serious waste of effort.

B. *Technical Quality*

1. Is the design as *sophisticated* as possible given resources?

Sophistication refers to the extent to which the evaluation plan provides control over possible contaminating variables (factors that might obscure or compete with program effects), while not sacrificing representativeness (the manner in which the program will be realized in the real world) (Snow, 1974). Thus a field experiment, where certain competing variables are controlled and some randomization is possible, is probably more sophisticated than a non-randomized, pre-post case study of one school. This is not to say, however, that sophistication is the *sine qua non* of evaluation criteria; nor that non-randomized case studies are always lacking in sophistication. There are ways, as we have described in Section III, to bolster the sophistication of various types of evaluation designs.

2. Are there provisions for *quality control?*

Quality control of an evaluation is achieved through careful monitoring of data collection, analysis, and reporting. Careful monitoring often involves collecting more data than ultimately will be needed for a technical report, data such as anecdotal commentary from participants, videotapes to supplement classroom field notes, and so on. It may also include strict standardization of procedures (in test administration, interviewing, and the like), and special training of evaluation staff. Quality control in analysis and reporting concerns cross-checking numbers, examining data in a variety of ways, portraying effects from several angles (in tables, figures, words), and being careful to see that no misrepresentation or data omissions occur ("sins of commission and omission"; Dunkin and Biddle, 1974).

3. Are conclusions *warranted* by the data?

Accurate interpretation of data may be the most significant criterion of a good evaluation, since it represents the basis for actual decisions. When interpretations "go beyond the data" or attempt to draw unwarranted implications, the evaluation may be used to justify improper practice. Evaluators can guard against inappropriate interpretation by linking all conclusions directly to the data at hand and formally noting the limitations of the study. For example, evaluation results of a staff development program initiated by one principal should not be applied to all administrators. Nor do results found in one school district generalize to another without proper sampling or justification.

C. *Utility*

1. Are results *clearly reported* and *distributed* to all users at a time when they will be useful for decision making?
Clear reporting dictates that technical *and* non-technical reports should be written in concise fashion, while still managing to cover important aspects of the evaluation. Reports should be distributed to all present and potential users. In the case of a staff development evaluation, reports might be distributed to an audience as general as users of the ERIC system, as well as a more specific audience, such as parents. Further, evaluation efforts are useful to the extent that reports reach decision makers in time to influence decision making.

2. Are results clearly *related* to major questions?
Evaluation results should address the original evaluation questions. This is what some writers refer to as "prioritizing" results. Many results, including unexpected ones, are obtained in an evaluation; these ought not to be ignored. But "priority" results are those that speak directly to the questions with which the evaluation began.

D. *Propriety*

1. Are *responsibilities* of all constituents stated explicitly?
This criterion pertains to evaluation consumers. They should possess sufficient information about what is required to duplicate the effort, as nearly as possible, elsewhere. Statements of responsibilities for all involved parties help ensure replicability. Lists of responsibilities for teachers, principals, and so on may even be taken directly from evaluation reports and distributed as guidelines to individuals about to embark on the same program.

2. Are participants *consulted* and *informed* throughout the process?
As mentioned previously, participants' rights include the right to consultation and information. This is particularly important in evaluation, where results can easily be compromised by unwilling or uninvolved participants, and where outcomes are used for decision making. Generally speaking, involving participants from the beginning—at the earliest planning stage—is recommended, as are provisions for keeping participants informed throughout the study. Simple bulletins or brief meetings may be sufficient to maintain information flow and prevent participants from withdrawing their support.

3. Are all expenditures *justified* and *public?*
Here again, the importance of careful monitoring and reporting cannot
be overstressed. Consumers' rights obligate evaluators to make available
all information concerning public spending.

V. Conclusion

We have tried in the preceding pages to examine staff development
evaluation as an organizational process involving decision making, goals,
quality control, and compromises based on scarce resources. We have employed sets of questions directed at evaluation planners to cover such
topics as the criteria of good evaluations and ways to modify evaluation
designs in light of constraints. This format underscores our belief that
evaluation design can best be regarded as a decision-making process in
which certain basic questions must be addressed.

According to decision theorists, the likelihood of making the "best"
decision for a given situation is increased when decision makers have a
clear conception of the intended outcomes (goals) and access to information on various alternative courses of action. In the spirit of maximizing
the quality of evaluation decisions, we have discussed the possible goals
of evaluation and alternative ways to collect and analyze evaluation information. While recognizing that many of the terms and concepts presented in the chapter are technical, we hope that persons without formal
evaluation training will find the discussion useful, at best, in planning
and conducting staff development evaluations and, at least, in discovering areas they might pursue further.

Up to this point we have written as if the value of formal evaluations was beyond question. In closing, however, we wish to sound a cau-
tionary note. Evaluations should not be regarded as universally useful or
necessary undertakings. Done in a hasty, unsystematic, or insensitive manner, staff development evaluations have the potential to leave schools in
worse condition than they were in before the evaluations. In an earlier
study, one of us (Duke, 1978) identified a variety of possible "negative
by-products" of evaluation. These included the encouragement of faculty
distrust of evaluations, teacher anxiety and low morale, over-testing subjects, and manipulation of local educational goals. Evaluators must remind themselves that the scientific demands for high quality data and

the political exigencies of their work are not legitimate excuses for unethical or uncaring conduct.

REFERENCES

Bem, D. J. *Beliefs, Attitudes, and Human Affairs.* Belmont, Calif.: Brooks/Cole, 1970.

Campbell, D. T., and Stanley, J. C. *Experimental and Quasi-Experimental Designs for Research.* Skokie, Ill.: Rand, McNally, 1966.

Cooley, W. W., and Lohnes, P. R. *Evaluation Research in Education.* New York: John Wiley, 1976.

Cronbach, L. J. "Beyond the Two Disciplines of Scientific Psychology." *American Psychologist* 30 (1975) : 116-126.

Cronbach, L. J. *Educational Psychology,* 3rd ed. New York: Harcourt, Brace, Jovanovich, 1977.

Cronbach, L. J. *Research on Classrooms and Schools: Formulation of Questions, Design, and Analysis.* Stanford, Calif.: Stanford Evaluation Consortium, 1978.

Cronbach, L. J.; Ambron S.; Dornbusch, S. M.; Hess, R. D.; Hornik, R. C.; Phillips, D. C.; Walker, D. F.; and Weiner, S. P. *Evaluation for an Open Society: Aims, Methods, and Institutional Arrangements.* San Francisco: Jossey-Bass, in press.

Duke, Daniel L. "Toward Responsible Innovation." *The Educational Forum* 42 (1978) : 351-372.

Dunkin, M. J., and Biddle, B. J. *The Study of Teaching.* New York: Holt, Rinehart, and Winston, 1974.

Eisner, E. W. "On the Uses of Educational Connoisseurship and Criticism for Evaluating Classroom Life." *Teachers College Record* 78,3 (1977) : 345-358.

Fullan, M., and Pomfret, A. "Research on Curriculum and Instruction Implementation." *Review of Educational Research* 47,2 (1977) : 335-397.

Griffin, G. A. "Guidelines for the Evaluation of Staff-Development Programs." *Teachers College Record* 80,1 (1978) : 126-139.

Guba, E. G. "Problems in Utilizing the Results of Evaluation." *Journal of Research and Development in Education* 8,3 (1975) : 42-54.

Guba, E. G.; Ridings, J. M.; and Stufflebeam, D. L. "A Progress Report on the Project to Develop Standards for Educational Evaluation." Paper presented at the Annual Meeting of the American Educational Research Association, San Francisco, 1979.

Holsti, O. R. *Content Analysis for the Social Sciences and Humanities.* Reading, Mass.: Addison-Wesley, 1969.

Joyce, B. R., and Showers, B. "Improving Inservice Training: The Messages of Research." *Educational Leadership* 37,5 (1980) : 379-385.

Scriven, Michael. "Pros and Cons About Goal-Free Evaluation." *Evaluation Comment* 3 (1972) : 1-4.

Snow, R. E. "Representative and Quasi-Representative Designs for Research on Teaching." *Review of Educational Research* 44 (1974) : 265-291.

Stallings, J. A. *Learning to Look.* Belmont, Calif.: Wadsworth, 1977.

Stufflebeam, D. L., et al. *Educational Evaluation and Decision-Making.* Itasca, Ill.: Peacock, 1971.

Thomas, W. I., and Thomas, E. S. *The Child in America.* New York: Knopf, 1928.

Weiss, C. H. *Evaluation Research.* Englewood Cliffs, N.J.: Prentice-Hall, 1972.

6

A Memorandum for the Future
Bruce Joyce

BRUCE JOYCE DESCRIBES a staff development scenario for the future in Chapter 6. This scenario is not startlingly different from what is currently present in many quality school systems today. What is important about it, perhaps, is that it is *not* startlingly different or unusual, but that it reflects a healthy and natural institutionalization of growth and improvement.

He points toward the time (not too far distant) when the teacher— and all others who work in schools—will routinely recognize the need to grow and change, will go about it without a great deal of fuss, and will have a genuine feeling of satisfaction in the process.

BETWEEN 1940 AND 1970, American education expanded with incredible rapidity. The teaching force increased from about one million persons to over two million. Mass production came to teacher education to fill the demand for credentialled personnel. Schools of education were enlarged not only to match the size of the demand but became much larger, for one-third of preservice graduates never sought employment as teachers and another third accepted teaching jobs but voluntarily left the profession within three years. Schools of education operated with new and inexperienced faculties whose energy was consumed with teaching and supervising the large number of teacher candidates generated by expansion. The time of professional preparation was brief and the circumstances were chaotic (Joyce, Yarger, and Howey, 1977).

School districts opened schools at a very rapid rate, often promoting teachers, counselors, and others with little experience to principalships and asking them to weld beginning teachers into the faculties of these new schools.

Simultaneously, the suburbs drained whites from the cities, Gunnar Myrdal's (1944) prophetic "American Dilemma" became a nightmare of segregated races, and the urban school systems slid out from the control of social planners.

The public became alarmed. Soviet achievements, Communist threats, inner city problems, the alienation of youth in suburbia, children's increased fascination with television and their lessened interest in books and numbers, and the disadvantages of the caste system were all laid at the door of education. Wealthy suburbs and small cities protected their educational oases lest the surrounding confusion overwhelm them.

By 1970 the pace of expansion had slowed. Educators began to age in service, and the school population began to shrink. Calls for economy joined cries for quality to become a major public issue. An aroused citizenry, appalled by the changes that had occurred in America, came to believe that schools were not only ineffective but cost too much. Teachers organizations became tougher and more unified over economic issues in order to increase their power in the struggle with public opinion. Among professional educators talk of "burn-out" rose. Teachers and administrators alike became urgently aware of their need for replenishment and nurturance. Frequently suspicious of one another and unsure that universities could help, many became angry about the state of inservice education and about their working conditions. Supervisors and curriculum specialists became concerned that the environment for professional growth had serious shortcomings in *most* places.

And so was born the present concern with staff development. The question emerged, "How can we create a professionwide environment which will enrich the lives of teachers and administrators, help faculties and districts enliven and continuously improve their schools, and ensure that each education professional continuously studies and enhances his or her craft?"

A History of Riches

Despite the problems besetting education, we do not come to the topic of staff development with an empty storehouse of ideas or information. The period in which schooling expanded so rapidly and optimistically was also the richest period of experimentation and development in the history of the common school. A large community of researchers was developed and techniques for conducting studies of teaching and learning were vastly improved (Gage, 1977; Medley, 1977). Researchers, developers, teachers, school districts, and federal and state governments generated substantial innovative efforts that have yielded a great deal of information about teaching and schooling and how they might (and might not) be improved (Joyce and Morine, 1977).

The Reform Movements

In the last 25 years there have been unprecedented attempts to improve American education. Well before Sputnik, the schools were being attacked for failing to teach the basic skills. Rudolf Flesch's book *Why Johnny Can't Read* was quickly followed by suggestions that Ivan *could*. Sputnik increased the concern that young Americans were not acquiring the advanced academic training necessary for the competitive international life required in a technological age. The academic reform movement (Joyce and Morine, 1977) was developed and the New Physics, New Mathematics, and other efforts to bring the work of advanced scholars into the classroom met with excitement and controversy. These academic reforms generated their own species of concern: parents worried that the content of schooling would be too unfamiliar to them, and teachers faced the problem of studying the disciplines afresh and learning new and unfamiliar teaching strategies.

Contemporaneously with the academic reform movement questions were raised about whether the organization of schools was the best we could have. Team teaching was generated along with a considerable variety of alternative forms of what came to be known as "differentiated staffing." The notion that teachers should work in teams with specialized functions and study their craft continuously and rigorously arose and was accepted in many quarters. Robert Schaefer's (1967) succinct statement in *The School as a Center of Inquiry* summarized the dilemma of teaching as one of operating from continuously incomplete knowledge, a state which he reasoned is best remedied by organizations in which teachers are teamed to experiment continuously with their teaching, trying out different frames of reference for looking at students and experimenting with methods—tinkering with them to make them work. Schaefer also pointed out the importance of inservice education being continuous. As he put it, "we cannot wind the teacher up like an old Victrola and expect him to play sweet, cerebral music forever." Thus, with team teaching came the idea of the clinical study of teaching, beginning the movement known as clinical supervision (Hunter, 1967, 1971, 1980).

Along with these movements architects began to design schools to accommodate the new organizational forms and teaching styles. Some of these schools were built around definite philosophies of teaching (for example, the Valley Winds School in Riverview Gardens, Missouri, was built around concepts of multimedia storage and retrieval systems and flexible learning spaces). Other schools emphasized learning centers which could be reoriented as philosophies of schooling changed.

The mid-60s saw a large number of social reforms come into existence. How should the schools teach about Communism? (Should they teach what is good about it, what is bad about it, or avoid it?) The movement to integrate society through redistricting of school districts began, facing schools with the need to try to reunite the divided society by helping children in diverse communities learn to relate to each other. Close behind integration came multicultural education to help each student understand his/her heritage and that of fellow students. Mainstreaming came into existence to try to integrate handicapped children into the socializing forces of the school.

Technical reforms also came about. In Hagerstown, Maryland, a major experiment was carried on to bring television massively into the classroom. In the Midwest an airplane carrying a television antenna beamed messages to the classrooms in that vast area. Multimedia data storage and retrieval systems were developed as well as multimedia learning systems. Computer-managed systems such as IPI came into existence. Simulators were built and simulation games were sent to the schools. In teacher education, innovations such as "mini-courses" and the use of interaction analysis proliferated rapidly.

Other reforms were based on the needs of society. Should schools teach "law and order" principles directly or engage in sophisticated forms of moral education? Along with the move toward accountability and mastery learning, competency-based education was developed. Dissatisfaction with decision making and community relations produced the "organization development" movement.

While all this was going on there were very broad social changes which affected the schools tremendously. Sheer population increase impacted the educational system. As mentioned earlier, in the 50s and early 60s schools proliferated rapidly and hundreds of thousands of new teachers joined their faculties. By the late 60s the expansion of schools stopped abruptly and a once young profession turned into an aging cadre of experienced teachers talking about fatigue and boredom. Simultaneously the public which had sought and encouraged alternative forms of schooling became frightened and gradually transformed its support into a nervous suspicion.

Changes brought about by the school improvement movements gradually eroded. John Goodlad and Frances Klein's *Looking Behind the Classroom Door* (1971) describes the scene in the 70s as one in which there are only residual effects of the vast number of reform movements. The normative bands of schooling have closed around the alternatives and squeezed most of them out.

Yet, we can learn a great deal from the reforms period. We know that it is easier to bring new materials to schools than to generate new teaching processes (Fullan and Pomfret, 1977). Changes that require new organization are much more difficult to implement than those that fit comfortably into the normative structure of organizations. Community support and joint "ownership" of innovations are essential for implementation.

What these lessons boil down to is that *substantial, continuous staff development is essential to the improvement of schooling and, equally important, to the development of the capability for the continuous renewal of education.* A static school is a dying school. Staff development is one essential ingredient of a lively, dynamic school that improves itself through the release of a self-feeding energy born of the quest for understanding about how creative teaching and learning can best take place.

We know very well how to change schools. Energetic people working skillfully from a technical point of view and carefully from a political point of view can bring about almost any alternative model of schooling that has yet been invented. We know also that these changes, once brought about, will not persist unless there is a sustained effort and the organization is carefully developed. We know much better how to bring about changes than how to sustain them.

Also we know that almost any change will be opposed by some faction or group within the profession or community unless it is understandable to them and they share in the planning process. Thus, "ownership" of changes is critical if they are to be implemented without chaos and sustained without discomfort. Bringing about the involvement of the community and an environment which sustains professional growth are the major tasks of our time.

A New Fundamentalism

Schools have been strong enough to absorb new personnel in vast numbers and withstand enormous social upheaval. What has resulted, however, is a profession that is exceedingly troubled at present.

If the education profession is to flourish and if schools are to be a vital force in society, it is necessary to rebuild the school into a lifelong learning laboratory not only for children but for teachers as well. The improvement of staff development is not a matter of deciding how to create and implement ad hoc programs. Rather, it is a matter of generating a rich environment in which every education professional becomes a student of education and works continuously to improve his or her skills. If schools are not being improved, they atrophy. Teaching is an experiment in life and, like a marriage, it must be worked on or it will become desperately routine. The environment of the school must re-generate the relationships between teachers, learners, and community members or the school will lose its vitality.

Making schools into learning laboratories will be a long, slow process, but it is time for us to make the commitment and to put our energies into that process and not waste them by repeating the mistakes of the past.

The primary task in staff development is to develop a professional, growth-oriented ecology in all schools. The purposes are three:

1. To enrich the lives of teachers and school administrators so that they continuously expand their general education, their emotional range, and their understanding of children.

2. To generate continuous efforts to improve schools. School faculties, administrators, and community members need to work together to make their schools better and acquire the knowledge and skills necessary to bring those improvements into existence.

3. To create conditions which enable professional skill development to be continuous. Every teacher and administrator needs to be a student of learning and teaching and to engage in a continuous process of experimentation with their behavior and that of their students. Each education professional needs to study alternative approaches to schooling and teaching, to select ones which will expand their capabilities and to acquire the understanding and skills necessary to make fresh alternatives a part of their ongoing repertoire of professional competence.

The Knowledge Base

The array of available experience and research-based knowledge does not by any means add up to a complete, tested paradigm for building either comprehensive staff development systems or implementing short-term programs. However, it is important to use what is available. The chapters in this yearbook synthesize this knowledge from several perspectives.

In Chapter Two, Bents and Howey present frameworks from which we can approach adult learning. They believe that education professionals can both study their preferred learning styles and expand their ability to exploit a wider range of learning opportunities. In other words, they provide a basis on which professionals can begin to study how they learn and why. Essentially, *learning how to learn* should be a major aspect of staff development.

In Chapter Three, Roark and Davis bring together the literature on organization development and suggest its applications to staff development. Most important, the study of organizational behavior can itself be a significant part of the substance of inservice education. In other words, school personnel are members of organizations and the health of organizations greatly affects the effectiveness of individuals as well as the vigor of collective activity. Roark and Davis suggest that teachers and administrators can study the human systems to which they belong and can systematically improve those systems. While OD theory does not provide complete, sure-fire formulas for making organizations perfect, its concepts and knowledge provide a strong framework from which to begin.

In Chapter Four, Wood, Thompson, and Russell synthesize research and opinion from a large number of sources to present us with a plan for designing and implementing inservice programs. Their approach gives us an example of an essential aspect of planning—defining the multiple dimensions of the problem of generating staff development environments and sifting through the knowledge base to develop operational strategies.

In Chapter Five, Duke and Corno examine paradigms for designing the evaluation of staff development systems and initiatives. They approach the task of embedding evaluation components in the effort to improve both the overall environment of staff development and the initiation of specific thrusts.

In addition to the research and experience which these authors have assembled we can draw on the history of the "reform movements" and several recent investigations, some of which approached inservice education and others which yielded useful information even though they were targeted on other areas. These include:

—A nationwide survey of preservice teacher education (Joyce, Yarger, and Howey, 1977)

—A study of inservice teacher education in which interviews were conducted with more than 1500 persons concerned with staff development and 30 position papers were commissioned and analyzed (Joyce and others, 1976)

—A study of the National Urban/Rural School Development Program which capitalized on the energy of school community councils to generate plans and staff development activities to accompany them (Joyce, 1978)

—An extensive series of studies of teachers' thinking in classrooms (McNair and Joyce, 1978-79)

—A series of surveys of inservice teacher education practices in several states (Yarger and others, 1980)

—A study of initiatives in staff development at the federal and state levels and the impact of those initiatives in several local school sites in California (Joyce, 1980)

—Investigations into the relationship between teachers' psychological states and their use of staff development activities (McKibbin and Joyce, 1980)

—The literature on preservice and inservice training research (Joyce and Showers, 1980)

—The literature on organizational and curricular change in education (Hall and others, 1975; Fullan and Pomfret, 1977; Joyce and others, 1980).

This list by itself indicates the complexity of staff development. The substance of the studies enlarges the picture of complexity.

Resources

Although the area is in need of organization and fiscal support, there are many resources which apparently are not used optimally. Speaking of the nation as a whole the more than 1400 institutions which offer preservice teacher preparation also offer courses which are taken by inservice personnel. There are presently more than 45,000 education professors who do or potentially could render such service. There is about an equal number of supervisors and curriculum consultants employed by public school districts, part of whose function is also to render service. Combined, there are close to 100,000 professors and curriculum consultants and about two million classroom teachers, or, approximately one professor and consultant for every 20 teachers. To be sure, the professor/consultant group does not work full time to provide services, but nonetheless there are many persons who bear a service relationship to education personnel. As we will see later, there is considerable dissatisfaction with the services presently being rendered by both university and school system personnel but their numbers and the potential service they can render cannot be denied.

In addition, there are about 100,000 principals and vice-principals employed in the 17,000 school districts in the nation, again about one for every 20 classroom teachers. From the point of view of many experts in inservice education, one of the major tasks of the building-level administrator is to assist teachers to grow in professional competence or to help teachers organize staff development programs tailored to their needs. If each building-level administrator spent ten percent of his or her time in staff development-related activities, the total effort would be enormous.

We must also consider the nearly 50,000 non-supervisory instructional personnel (reading instructors, media and communication experts, mental health specialists, and department chairpersons) who are also expected to act at least in part as support personnel for teachers.

In addition, teachers can become effective and powerful trainers of one another. (In fact, most inservice education *should* be carried out by the two million education professionals who presently work in classrooms.) Added to these reservoirs of people is the vast fund of alternative approaches to teaching and learning generated during the last 30 years. There is no lack of things to study. Hence, there is plenty of substance to deal with and resources with which to approach the job.

Realities

At present "realities" are often used as an excuse for inaction. Actually, knowledge of the realities of schooling should provide us with the understanding necessary to direct our efforts deftly and in many cases give us springboards to action.

Privatism: Kevin Ryan put it very well when he said that "teaching is the second most private social activity." Traditionally, teachers teach in isolation from one another. The average teacher visits other teachers to observe them teach less frequently than once every three years (Yarger and others, 1980). The effect of this privatism is that many teachers have no concept of who they are professionally or how they stack up against others. The following is an account from an experienced staff development specialist.

In my life I regularly encounter teachers who do certain kinds of things superbly. The other day I was working with a school faculty which I knew very well. One teacher in that faculty does a particular kind of thing skillfully and fluidly, while most of the other members of the faculty labor at it awkwardly. I asked that teacher to demonstrate that practice to the others and she was very uncomfortable with my suggestion. "I'm simply not that good," she said. "But you are," I said. "I'm just an average teacher," she replied. "Well that may or may not be true," I replied in my turn, "but you do this particular kind of thing much better than anyone else in the faculty." She simply was totally reluctant to believe me. I was able to persuade her and she was amazed at the approval she received from her fellow faculty members.

Because most teachers don't see others work they have no idea what they do well and what they do poorly. The average person does some things with considerable skill while other acts require considerable labor. When teachers observe each other they know where they stand and what they can learn from each other. Furthermore, not knowing who they are or where they stand makes it difficult for them to have adequate, realistic self-concepts as professionals. Some people who are very good at some tasks are uncertain and insecure, while others who are rather awkward in many aspects of teaching think they are relatively skillful. Considerable anxiety is generated by the privatism and there is great loss in terms of possible learning from one another.

Cynicism: In inservice education, cynicism appears in two ways which cause considerable difficulty. The first is the view that most inservice education is not very helpful. Thus, well-planned and effective inservice education programs have to struggle against the reputation of their predecessors. Second, some categories of people have little credibility as trainers. Many teachers think that university professors do not make effective inservice educators. In recent surveys it has been found that they have even less confidence in supervisors and building administrators (Yarger and others, 1980). Teachers say they prefer each other as trainers. Yet, teachers who have served in the training role frequently report that they have as much difficulty in establishing credibility as do persons in other roles in education (Joyce and others, 1976). Ultimately, if staff development is to succeed, professionals will have to trust and help one another, rather than react cynically.

Lack of experience with the powerful training options: One reason for the lack of confidence in inservice education is that many educators have never experienced really effective and powerful training. In order to learn new teaching strategies, teachers need to study theory, see demonstrations, have opportunities for practice with careful feedback, and, finally, receive coaching on site (Joyce and Showers, 1980). Very few people receive or deliver inservice education which combines all of these elements. We need professionwide retraining incorporating these powerful elements.

Developing problem-solving modalities: Faculties vary greatly in the ways they work with one another. Some faculties can easily and comfortably attack problems. More often, the privatism in teaching divides teachers from one another. Where a powerful problem-solving approach is developed, curriculum redevelopment, mutuality in the study of teaching, and support of the social climate are much easier to bring about. The nature of the social system in the school greatly affects the impact of initiatives to improve it (Joyce, 1980).

Initial training: The clinical aspects of preservice teacher education are incredibly short (Howey, Yarger, and Joyce, 1978). When we compare teacher training to preparation for the trades, the clinical experiences teachers receive (the combination of professional courses and student teaching) occupy only from 16 to 26 weeks of full-time training. This is substantially less than training for trades such as hairdressing. In addition, the theoretical and problem-solving components of teacher education programs are generally inarticulated. The theory that is studied is often not seen in practice and many student teachers do not get a chance to try out the ideas that they received in theory or methods courses.

Teachers learn to teach on-the-job and the on-the-job conditions are both demanding and chaotic. The level of skill that most teachers achieve depends on their independent ability to solve problems in the situation rather than as a result of their professional training program. Very few teachers are familiar with the alternative models of teaching available to them and fewer still have on-the-job assistance in mastering them.

Pressures toward normative teaching: In addition, teachers are pressured toward the recitation style that dominates the education profession (Hoetker and Albrand, 1969). Trying alternatives is a risky business. For one thing, when teachers explore a new teaching strategy, their performance suffers in that they are less comfortable with the new than with the old (Joyce and Weil, 1980; Joyce, 1980). Second, students are uncomfortable with novel approaches to teaching and tend to pressure teachers back toward more familiar modalities. Finally, other teachers and community members are suspicious of awkwardness in performance. However, initial awkwardness is a condition of the acquisition of a new teaching approach. A social climate that encourages risk-taking and provides a protective haven in which to experiment with teaching is essential in order to combat the pressures that strip the profession of lively alternatives in favor of the normative mode.

Self-concept: Like all other human beings, teachers have self-concepts. Persons in the self-actualizing state reach out to develop themselves and explore more alternatives with their students. Persons at a survival or competency stage tend not to reach out. It is essential that the environment of the school pull professionals toward a self-actualizing state (McKibbin and Joyce, 1980).

These are the realities. Staff development programs must overcome privatism, foster self-actualizing within a problem-solving mode, use the more powerful training modalities, and help teachers resist the pressures which reduce teaching to a normative activity.

Ideas: Propositions for Action

Everyone a Student of Teaching

Every teacher and school administrator needs to be a student of teaching in a public, cumulative fashion. No matter how competent teachers are, they, like actors, need to study their profession regularly, looking for new options, polishing the skills they possess, developing new ones, rethinking the curriculum of the schools in which they work, and making the learning environments of schools more powerful (Joyce and Weil, 1980).

Applying the Research on Training

Research on training has given us several working hypotheses for program construction:

The first message from that research is very positive: teachers are wonderful learners. Nearly all teachers can acquire new skills that "fine tune" their competence. They can also learn a considerable repertoire of teaching strategies that are new to them.

The second message is more sobering, but still optimistic: in order to improve their skills and learn new approaches to teaching, teachers need certain conditions—conditions that are not common in most inservice settings even when teachers participate in the governance of those settings.

The third message is also encouraging: the research base reveals what conditions help teachers to learn. This information can be used to design staff development activities for classroom personnel (Joyce and Showers, 1980).

The "conditions" referred to above consist of five training elements. If all five elements are combined, it is likely there will be satisfaction with the training, and the skills which are its objective will transfer into the working repertoire of the professional. The elements are:

1. Presentation of theory or description of skill or strategy
2. Modeling or demonstration of skills or models of teaching

3. Practice in simulated and classroom settings

4. Structured and open-ended feedback (provision of information about performance)

5. Coaching for application (hands-on, in-classroom assistance with the transfer of skills and strategies to the classroom).

The most effective training activities, then, will be those that combine theory, modeling, practice, feedback, and coaching to application. The knowledge base seems firm enough that we can predict that if those components are in fact combined in inservice programs, we can expect the outcomes to be considerable at all levels (Joyce and Showers, 1980).

Everyone a Trainer

If the more powerful training options are to be implemented teachers have to become trainers of one another—helping everyone to learn to study theory, to demonstrate, to organize and practice, give feedback, and, of critical importance, to coach one another in the classroom. Teachers themselves are the most valuable resource. Building their capability to coach one another is vital in the development of productive staff development.

Sharing Power Increases Power

Both the Rand Corporation studies of federally-funded programs designed to generate local innovative power (Berman, 1976) and the evaluation of the Urban/Rural School Development Program point to the importance of collaboration among teachers, administrators, and community members both for the improvement of schools and the creation of vital environments for professional growth.

Most important is the decision to redirect personnel and material resources toward the reconstruction of the ecology of the school, building cooperation between teachers, school administrators, staff developers, university personnel, and community members. Over time, several changes need to be brought about which capitalize on our experience and the research base which we presently possess:

Governance. Establish school/community councils, bringing together teachers, school administrators, and community members in each local school or cluster of schools to engage in the process of school improvement and the redevelopment of inservice training.

Training. Create a professionwide movement to help all personnel increase their capability to use the more powerful training options. Of critical importance is the preparation of teachers and local building administrators to engage in the continuous, vital coaching process.

The Faculty as a Self-Study Unit. Each faculty needs to engage in the study of the environments they live in, determining ways to improve them and building relationships around a self-actualizing norm. The profession cannot survive divided. Each faculty needs to seek ways to break down the privatism of the classroom and the divisions that presently exist between teachers and school administrators and create a climate in which risk-taking and problem-solving are the norm. Within that environment they, supported by the school community council, should develop a continuous school improvement plan.

Job-Embedded Inservice. Time needs to be built into the school calendar so that teams can engage in the study of one another's teaching and carry out the coaching element that is essential to the improvement of professional skills. University and district personnel can bring new ideas to the school and help teachers learn to train each other. Education is an experiment in living which brings teachers and learners together to explore possibilities and find meaningful lives in their society. The ecology of the school needs to be shaped to generate a situation in which teachers and learners try the rich array of approaches to learning that are our legacy from the past and create the new schools of tomorrow that will be society's inheritance from us.

REFERENCES

Beran, Paul, et al. *Federal Programs Supporting Education Change, Vol. X: Executive Summary.* Santa Monica, Calif.: Rand, 1976.

Fullan, Michael, and Pomfret, Allan. "Research on Curriculum and Instruction Implementation." *Review of Educational Research* 47 (Spring 1977) : 335-397.

Gage, N. L. *The Scientific Basis for the Art of Teaching.* New York: Teachers College Press, 1979.

Goodlad, John, and Klein, Frances M. *Looking Behind the Classroom Door.* New York: McGraw-Hill, 1971.

Hall, Gene E., et al. "Levels of Use of the Innovation: A Framework for Analyzing Innovation Adoption." *Journal of Teacher Education* 26 (Spring 1975) : 52-56.

Hoetker, J., and Albrand, W. "The Persistence of the Recitation." *American Educational Research Journal* 1 (1969) : 145-167.

Howey, Kenneth R.; Yarger, Sam; and Joyce, Bruce R. *Improving Teacher Education.* Washington, D.C.: Association of Teacher Educators, 1978.

Hunter, Madeline. "The Learning Process." In *Handbook for Teachers.* Edited by Eli Seifman and Dwight Allen. Glenview, Ill.: Scott-Foresman, 1971.

Hunter, Madeline. *Motivation Theory for Teachers.* El Segundo, Calif.: TIP Publications, 1967.

Hunter, Madeline. "Six Types of Supervisory Conferences." *Educational Leadership* 37 (February 1980) : 408-412.

Joyce, Bruce R. "The Ecology of Staff Development." Paper Presented to the Annual Meeting of the American Educational Research Association, Boston, 1980.

Joyce, Bruce R. *Lessons Learned from the History of Change.* Omaha: University of Nebraska Press, 1980.

Joyce, Bruce R. "The Social Ecology of the School: Dynamics of the Inter/External Systems." Paper Presented to the Annual Meeting of the American Educational Research Association, Boston, 1980.

Joyce, Bruce R., ed. *Flexibility in Teaching.* New York: Longman, 1980.

Joyce, Bruce R., ed. *Involvement: A Shared Governance of Teacher Education.* Syracuse: National Dissemination Center, 1978.

Joyce, Bruce R., et al. *ISTE Report Volume I: Issues to Face.* Syracuse: National Dissemination Center, 1976.

Joyce, Bruce R., and Morine, Greta. *Creating the School.* Boston: Little, Brown, 1977.

Joyce, Bruce R., and Showers, Beverly. "Improving Inservice Training: The Messages of Research." *Educational Leadership* 37 (February 1980) : 379.

Joyce, Bruce R., and Weil, Marsha. *Models of Teaching,* 2nd ed. Englewood Cliffs, N.J.: Prentice-Hall, 1980.

Joyce, Bruce R.; Yarger, Sam; and Howey, Kenneth. *Preservice Teacher Education.* Palo Alto, Calif.: Consolidated Publications, 1977.

McKibbin, Michael D., and Joyce, Bruce R. "The Teacher as Learner." *Theory Into Practice* (Fall 1980) .

McNair, Kathleen, and Joyce, Bruce R. "Thought and Action, A Frozen Section: The South Bay Study." *Educational Research Quarterly* 3 (Winter 1978-79) : 16-25.

Medley, Donald. *Teacher Competence and Teacher Effectiveness.* Washington, D.C.: American Association of Colleges for Teacher Education, 1977.

Myrdal, Gunnar. *The American Dilemma.* New York: Harper and Row, 1944.

Schaefer, Robert J. *The School as a Center of Inquiry.* New York: Harper and Row, 1967.

Yarger, Sam, et al. *Inservice Teacher Education.* Palo Alto, Calif.: Booksend Laboratory, 1980.

Making the Strange Familiar:
Scenes from a Future Teacher's Life
Bruce Joyce

THE ELEMENTS EXIST on which an exciting future can be built. Bill Gordon's felicitous phrase "making the strange familiar"* captures our task. Yet, we can envision a future which is really not all that strange in that nearly everything we can envision takes place in some form in quite a number of schools today. Our problem is to reconstruct the environments in which nearly all professionals work, so that the good ideas of today are released to operate everywhere, not only in a few places—so that a vibrant, synergistic environment for professional growth pervades the teaching profession. Good ideas abound and our methods for self-training are well-developed if not generally used. Let us suppose that we have changed the structure of the environment in a few large and many subtle ways. What would the environment then look like in the life of a mythical teacher just a few years into the future?

* * * * *

Brian Cavanaugh is the head of a teaching team responsible for much of the education of a group of eleven-year-olds. The school day begins with a brief meeting of the team to polish up the plans for the next day. The focus of the meeting is a science unit in which Brian is taking the part of the lead teacher. He has demonstrated a Cartesian Diver to the students the day before, working with small groups and leading them through Inquiry Training lessons designed to help them build and test hypotheses. One of the team members had watched him and has a number of suggestions.

"Brian, I'm not quite sure where you're going next. I'm having trouble planning my follow-up." Brian explains his purpose and makes a few suggestions for activities. One of the other teachers wants to discuss the inquiry skills of some of the students and has a suggestion for skill training that Brian can do with the whole group. The team members

*William Gordon, *Synectics* (Cambridge: Synectics, Inc., 1967).

128

touch base briefly about their activities in other curriculum areas and disband.

On the way home, Brian stops by the Teacher Center to pick up some materials that he will need for the rest of the week's activities. The science consultant is there and they spend a few minutes discussing how Brian's inquiry training work is going. The science consultant is released from her teaching team on a halftime basis this year to help other teachers in the science area and to work with the district curriculum committee. Brian tells her that he is still not totally comfortable with inquiry training and asks if she can drop by to watch him. "The other guys on the team have been helping me," he says, "but none of them has ever used inquiry training either and I need some expert criticism."

He arrives home before his wife or children do and uses the hour or so of quiet time to write a letter to his parents and one to the State Curriculum Resource Center asking for a bibliography of children's books on the Cultures of the South Pacific Islands. He's had difficulty locating enough books on that topic to support a social studies unit which he and his team have been planning. His wife Maryann returns and they catch up on each other's day while they change into their jogging clothes and take their evening run. By the time they get back to the house their children have come home and they prepare dinner and chat about the odds and ends of everyone's day. While they are doing the dishes he is interrupted by a call from the principal. "Brian, I'm sorry to bother you at home but I just remembered that you and I were going to visit the primary reading team tomorrow about 10 o'clock and I wondered if we could rearrange the observation to the afternoon?"

"I'm afraid not, I'm going to do another round of my inquiry training lessons and I've just arranged for one of the folks from the Teacher Center to come over and watch me work. It's not going badly but we're laboring somewhat and I could use that help."

"Okay, Brian, we'll keep our date at 10 o'clock. Something had come up but I'll just put it off, I think. We ought to keep our momentum going in the reading area."

The entire faculty is reworking the reading curriculum. Part of the program emphasizes literature and the other part uses computer-based instruction for training in skills. The primary team was the first to begin to use the computers and the intermediate teams are observing the process and preparing for the arrival of their own equipment. The computer programs are built around a game-type approach which includes embedded tests. Teachers and aides supervise the skill study times and most of the teachers' instructional time is spent helping individuals and small groups of children who have read literary selections.

Brian is responsible for helping his team use the computer terminals and, in turn, train their children to use them. Some of the primary teachers do not like the computerized approach at all while others appear to be very enthusiastic. The entire process is unfamiliar to most of the school faculty and the replacement of the traditional basal reading series by a part-literary/part-computerized approach has shaken up a good many parents as well. On the other hand, many of the students are used to calculators and computers in mathematics instruction and they are, on the whole, delighted with the whole approach.

The primary team spent much of the previous summer in a workshop in which the theory of the approach was explained and demonstrated with children attending a nearby summer school. Each of the teachers practiced working with a small group of students. The problem became one of getting the system in place. The whole faculty knew that unless they helped each other over the rough spots, they probably weren't going to get anywhere. They knew that every innovation made people uncomfortable and that they had to keep explaining the rationale to one another, continue to practice, and help the kids adjust to the new approach. The purpose of the visit was twofold; partly Charlie and Brian would be able to help the primary team figure out how to make things go smoother and partly they were getting ready for the job they would have with the other primary and the intermediate teams. Charlie and each of the team leaders were members of the school implementation team. All of them had been trained in clinical supervision and in techniques of training. Every teaching team worked on a particular emphasis each year. In the case of Brian's team this was the year to improve the science teaching and he and his staff were studying inquiry training and several other approaches to teaching. Reading was the thrust of the primary teams and would become the thrust of the intermediate teams during the next year.

The Cavanaugh children were old enough that breakfast was a relatively independent affair. Maryann and Brian took their morning run and had their coffee and toast to the accompaniment of "Good Morning World." On the way into the school Brian spent a few minutes having another cup of coffee with the special education resource teacher. A student with severe orthopedic handicaps had recently joined his team. The student had now learned that the optimistic talk about her recovery had not been well-founded and that she was likely to spend the rest of her life in a wheelchair or walking only with the aid of braces. She was, to put it mildly, extremely upset. The resource specialist was coaching Brian and the other teachers, teaching them about the nature of the disease, about the common emotional reactions when a child discovers how long-term her disability is going to be, and the most promising ways of helping her come to grips with her problem and deal productively with it. Brian and the resource teacher spent a few moments together each week, but he decided that more formal instruction would be useful. They set a date at a time when the teaching team ordinarily had their monthly dinner together and the resource specialist agreed to spend the evening with them and try to give them an overview of the kind of problem they were dealing with, her perceptions of the child, and the kind of information the other children need as they live and work with her.

At nine o'clock Brian introduces a group of 30 children to an area of literature that is new to them. He has brought along about 50 books of historical fiction. He talks about a number of them briefly, and helps the students to identify a variety of categories. Some of the books are biographies, some are narrative history, some describe life at various times in Europe, Asia, and America. He organizes the children into groups. Each child will read a number of the books and report to the others on them. After everyone has read a dozen or so books they will begin to form them into categories according to style and content. A number of the children have never read historical novels while others have read a good many. He takes a bit of time at the end of the session with the children who are wary and helps them find books he believes they will enjoy as the unit begins. Brian himself is an omniverous reader and has some trouble understanding why everybody doesn't like to read almost anything. Angie has sat in on his session. They spend a few minutes afterwards discussing how things went. She suggests that he read passages from a few books the next time they meet so that the children can have some idea about the flavor of the writing. She points out that much historical fiction makes grand adventure stories and that some of the students who are not initially turned on by history will find the adventure appealing.

By ten o'clock he and Charlie are with the primary team. The children are working with the computers and the aides are assisting them. It is very clear that there is a differential response to the method. Some of the children are racing through the skills sections, even children who have already mastered many of the skills appear to enjoy the process. The same is true for some of the children whose skills are less well developed. Other students flounder. A couple of the aides are positive and facilitative toward the method but one aide is relatively negative.

One of the teachers does not seem to know what to do to help the students. Both Charlie and Brian notice that there are three aides and three teachers in the area working with only 30 students. The other students assigned to the team are in another area with two teachers. It occurs to both of them that the team does not need all that personnel in that small space; some of them could be occupying their time better either planning or assembling materials. Both Brian and Charlie have been trained in Hunter's variation of clinical supervision, as have all the teachers in the school and the aides as well. Thus it is a surprise to no one when Charlie and Brian ask to meet with the aide and teacher respectively for a few minutes and then take a few minutes with the team as a whole to provide them with their impressions and to help the team analyze its planning and how it is using its personnel. Midge Skapone, the head of the team, is determined to make things go well and uses Brian and Charlie skillfully. She has noticed some of the same problems that they have, but understands very well that it is difficult to be a prophet in your own country, so she uses their feedback to help underline some of the points that she wishes to make. However, it has not occurred to her previously that they have actually overloaded the area with adult personnel. She realizes that her desire to have a successful implementation has probably caused her to overpopulate the space with teachers and aides.

Charlie has an early lunch at 11:30 and Brian joins him with the resource specialist in special education. All three of them have noticed that teachers and children alike are still displaying some phobic reactions to physically handicapped children and they decide to bring it up to the Policy Board. The resource specialist says, "I'd like to see us have a number of meetings in which specialists on various handicaps talk with us about the specific problems that handicapped children have. Physical handicaps, especially, are not nearly so scary once you get to know exactly what they are. Most teachers still don't know that blind and deaf children and the orthopedically handicapped all learn pretty much the same as anybody else and very few people realize how much they are able to compensate for their handicaps. Special education isn't nearly as 'special' as people think it is." Brian volunteers to bring the question up and says that he would like to do some demonstrations with her so that the faculty can get a clear idea about the real differences and similarities among the children.

He then hurries off to prepare his materials for the inquiry training lesson. As a result of their conversation in the morning, Charlie comes, as well as the representative from the Teacher Center. After the lesson is over they have a fifteen-minute clinical analysis and then Brian is off once again to the materials center for some items which she suggested. He arrives home with some time to read before Maryann gets home and they have their exercise.

*　　*　　*　　*　　*

Brian lives within a network of services. Some of these are directly present on the school site. He belongs to a council which includes the team leaders, the principal, and several community members who together are responsible for acting as a school improvement steering committee. They lead the faculty in the review of the curriculum, make plans to improve the organization of the school, and ensure that adequate training is available to help each teacher continuously work on skills and team functioning and deal with special problems as they arise. The council has been trained to analyze their decision-making processes and they have the services of a consultant from the district office. The district arranges for the local teaching resource center to provide a consultant in evaluation who helps them study the effects of the curriculum. Workshops offered jointly by the district, the local university, and the teacher center provide Brian and the other team leaders with training in clinical supervision. They in turn pass on this training to their teachers so that the entire school faculty is accustomed to observing one another and providing feedback.

When a curriculum change is made the teaching resource center offers training in the teaching strategies which are essential in the implementation of the curriculum change.

In addition, the teaching resource center and the local university jointly offer courses in alternative approaches to teaching. These are offered during the day. Teams arrange to free their members so that each person can take advantage of this opportunity to increase their teaching repertoire. At least two members of the school faculty form teams to attend these workshops so that they can coach one another as they return to the school and begin to experiment with the new approaches. The workshops follow the same training format described earlier. The new approaches to teaching are rationalized and demonstrated, practice is provided with peers and small groups of children, and the members of each school team are trained to coach one another as they experiment with the new procedures.

Also available to Brian is the on-site special education resource teacher who helps his team with children with special needs. For every six schools in the district there is also a consulting psychologist who is responsible for helping with diagnosis, offering special training to the teachers, and helping organize the evaluation of their progress.

A local university is responsible for offering sets of workshops on alternative approaches to each curriculum area. The principal attends monthly briefings on new developments and reports them to the council so that they can be aware of new developments which are taking place and select the ones that they will study. The local teaching center cooperates with the district to offer a continuous program of training for paid and volunteer aides and the teaching center staff offers mini-courses to parents on developmental psychology, building relationships with their children, and tutoring skills.

The district office is responsible for building, in conjunction with each local school council, an evaluation plan which is implemented on a continuous basis to provide a comparative picture of pupil progress within each school. These data are fed back to the school improvement councils so that they can assess the effectiveness of each of the dimensions of the school environment.

The school is organized into teaching teams for several reasons. First, it makes available to each child the services of several professionals. Second, it permits a differentiation of functions with team members taking turns being the "lead teacher" in each of the curriculum areas, so that the strengths of individuals can be capitalized on. Third, it provides flexibility in grouping for instruction. Fourth, it permits members of the teams to be freed weekly for three or four hours of direct inservice training (about as much as any given individual can absorb and adequately follow up).

Thus, Brian lives in a very rich environment. He has training in supervision and teacher training, studies organization development, participates in the continuous study of the curriculum areas, has help with children who have special needs, is near a curriculum resource center, and regularly studies new teaching strategies.

The governance structure provides for collaborative decision making by all members and training to improve that process itself. Community members are involved as paid and volunteer aides and serve as members of curriculum study groups so that they too can participate in and "own" changes that are made. The teachers vary in the extent to which they take advantage of the university courses which are offered. Brian is an omniverous learner and blocks out one afternoon each week, sometimes in courses in his specialties, and at other times in areas that simply interest him. The new set of units in the upper grade classes dealing with Far Eastern cultures is a direct result of a course that Brian and several of the other teachers took. The principal serves in many ways as the executive officer of the school improvement council. He does not attempt to impose changes unilaterally, nor does he shy away from initiative. An important part of his job is to keep up with curricular and instructional trends and to bring these to the attention of the council so that the constant scrutiny and improvement of the curriculum is embedded in the work of the school.

Most important, he has brought about a cooperative environment which stimulates the staff to improve their own skills as individuals and to reach out to improve the school as a whole.

Toward Naturalness

Every activity that Brian engaged in occurs commonly in a few schools and school districts somewhere in the United States. These particular activities have been chosen because of their naturalness—the extent to which they are embedded into his daily life as a teacher and team leader.

That quality of naturalness is our goal. We want to shape the environments in which we work so that opportunities for growing are a comfortable and inevitable part. An essential feature of this environment is a connection between professionals working together; the terrible isolation that has separated teachers from one another as they work will be ended. The line between teachers and administrators will diminish and all of them will know how to help each other. Their knowledge and the skill to back it up is another major difference. An investment will have been made in the capability of people to help one another study their performances and figure out ways of improving them.

Initiatives for improving the school and professional performance will continue to come from inside and outside. New ideas for teaching the academic subjects, new technologies, and new ways of working together will come from outside and also be transmitted from school to school as they are developed in the local scene. Faculties will continuously study their school and strive for ways to improve it, generating activities for their own growth as they go.

Until a professional growth environment has been developed most "models" for inservice education will be relatively weak for they will not come into an environment which can accept them confortably and capitalize on them powerfully. When a rigorous collegial environment has been developed models for staff development can acquire a richness and meaning far beyond what we have seen thus far in any but the most exceptional schools.

ASCD 1981 Yearbook
Committee and Authors

BETTY DILLON-PETERSON, Chairperson, ASCD 1981 Yearbook Committee; *Director of Staff Development, Lincoln Public Schools, Lincoln, Nebraska*

RICHARD H. BENTS, *Post-Doctoral Fellow, University of Maryland, College Park*

LYN CORNO, *Assistant Professor of Education, Stanford University, Stanford, California*

WALLACE E. DAVIS, JR., *Dean, College of Education, Corpus Christi State University, Corpus Christi, Texas*

DANIEL L. DUKE, *Assistant Professor of Education, Stanford University, Stanford, California*

KENNETH R. HOWEY, *Professor of Education and Assistant Chairperson, Department of Curriculum and Instruction, University of Minnesota, Minneapolis, Minnesota*

BRUCE JOYCE, *Booksend Laboratory, Palo Alto, California*

JAMES L. OLIVERO, *Association of California School Administrators, Newport Beach, California*

ALBERT E. ROARK, *Professor of Guidance and Counseling, University of Colorado, Boulder*

SISTER FRANCES RUSSELL, *Assistant Professor, Marywood College, Scranton, Pennsylvania*

STEVEN R. THOMPSON, *Assistant Director, Penn State/Keystone Central Teacher Corps Project, The Pennsylvania State University, University Park, Pennsylvania*

FRED H. WOOD, *Division Head, Division of Curriculum and Instruction, The Pennsylvania State University, University Park, Pennsylvania*

ELIZABETH YANCEY, *Vice Superintendent, District of Columbia Public Schools, Washington, D.C.*

ASCD Board of Directors

Executive Council, 1980-81

President:
BARBARA D. DAY, *Professor of Early Childhood Education, University of North Carolina, Chapel Hill*

President-Elect:
LUCILLE JORDAN, *Associate State Superintendent of Georgia Schools, State Department of Education, Atlanta, Georgia*

Immediate Past President:
BENJAMIN P. EBERSOLE, *Assistant Superintendent, Curriculum and Instructional Services, Board of Education of Baltimore County, Towson, Maryland*

JULIANNA L. BOUDREAUX, *Assistant Superintendent, Division of Instruction and Child Advocacy, New Orleans Public Schools, New Orleans, Louisiana*

GWYN BROWNLEE, *Director of Instructional Services Department, Education Service Center Region 10, Richardson, Texas*

LAWRENCE S. FINKEL, *Oceana Educational Communications, Dobbs Ferry, New York*

RAYMOND E. HENDEE, *Superintendent, Park Ridge School District #64, Park Ridge, Illinois*

ALICE VIVIAN HOUSTON, *Director of Curriculum Services Department, Oklahoma City, Oklahoma*

CAROLYN SUE HUGHES, *Consultant for Elementary Education, Parma City Schools, Parma, Ohio*

PHIL CLAYTON ROBINSON, *Principal, Clarence B. Sabbath School, River Rouge, Michigan*

139

MAIZIE R. SOLEM, *Instructional Planning Center, Sioux Falls Public Schools, Sioux Falls, South Dakota*

RONALD STODGHILL, *Deputy Superintendent of Instruction, St. Louis Public Schools, St. Louis, Missouri*

BOB TAYLOR, *Professor of Education, University of Colorado, Boulder, Colorado*

Board Members Elected at Large

(Listed alphabetically; the year in parentheses following each member's name indicates the end of the term of office.)

MITSUO ADACHI, *University of Hawaii, Honolulu* (1983)

MARTA M. BEQUER, *Dade County Public Schools, Miami, Florida* (1982)

REBA BURNHAM, *University of Georgia, Athens* (1981)

C. LOUIS CEDRONE, *Public Schools, Westwood, Massachusetts* (1983)

VIRGIE CHATTERGY, *University of Hawaii, Honolulu* (1981)

MILLY COWLES, *University of Alabama, Birmingham* (1982)

GLORIA COX, *Public Schools, Memphis, Tennessee* (1984)

MATTIE R. CROSSLEY, *Public Schools, Memphis, Tennessee* (1982)

JOAN D. KERELEJZA, *Public Schools, West Hartford, Connecticut* (1983)

MARCIA KNOLL, *Public Schools, Forest Hills, New York* (1984)

ARDELLE LLEWELLYN, *California State University, San Francisco* (1981)

ELIZABETH S. MANERA, *Arizona State University, Tempe* (1983)

GLORIA McFADDEN, *Oregon College of Education, Salem* (1984)

BLANCHE J. MARTIN, *Public Schools—Boone-Winnebago Counties, Rockford, Illinois* (1982)

MARVA GARNER MILLER, *Public Schools, Houston, Texas* (1983)

RONALD STODGHILL, *Public Schools, St. Louis, Missouri* (1981)

CLAIRE H. SULLIVAN, *Educational Consultant, Clearwater, Florida* (1984)

BOB TAYLOR, *University of Colorado, Boulder* (1981)

WILLIAM R. THOMAS, *Public Schools, Falls Church, Virginia* (1982)

MILDRED M. WILLIAMS, *State Department of Education, Jackson, Mississippi* (1984)

Unit Representatives to the Board of Directors

(Each Unit's President is listed first; other representatives follow in alphabetical order.)

Alabama:
BRANDON SPARKMAN, *Public Schools, Guntersville;* JAMES B. CONDRA, *University of Alabama, Gadsden;* JAMES GIDLEY, *Public Schools, Gadsden*

Alaska:
ANNA BETH BROWN, *Public Schools, Anchorage;* E. E. (GENE) DAVIS, *Public Schools, Anchorage*

Arizona:
LOIS FAIR WILSON, *Public Schools, Tucson;* PAT NASH, *University of Arizona, Tucson;* JULIE STRAND, *Public Schools, Tucson*

Arkansas:
JERRY DANIEL, *Public Schools, Camden;* PHILIP BESONEN, *University of Arkansas;* HAROLD MEASEL, *Pulaski County Special School District, Little Rock*

California:
ARTHUR COSTA, *California State University, Sacramento;* REGINA CAIN, *Public Schools, Tustin;* BOBBI MULHOLLAND, *Public Schools, Irvine;* DORIS PRINCE, *Public Schools, San Jose;* HELEN WALLACE, *Public Schools, Rohnert Park;* MARILYN WINTERS, *Public Schools, Woodland Hills*

Colorado:
JAMES F. CURRAN, *Public Schools, Englewood;* ROBERT ELLSPERMAN, *Boulder Valley School District, Boulder;* THOMAS MAGLARAS, *Adams-Arapahoe School District, Aurora*

Connecticut:
EDWARD H. BOURQUE, *Fairfield Public Schools, Southport;* BERNARD GOFFIN, *Public Schools, Monroe;* NELSON QUINBY, *Public Schools, West Redding*

Delaware:
CLAUDE E. SPENCER, *Public Schools, Wilmington;* MELVILLE WARREN, *Public Schools, Dover*

District of Columbia:
DOROTHY CHRISTIAN, *Public Schools, Washington;* PHYLLIS J. HOBSON, *Public Schools, Washington;* ANDREA J. IRBY, *Public Schools, Washington*

Florida:
CLAIRE H. SULLIVAN, *Education Consultant, Clearwater;* FRANK M. FARMER, *Public Schools, Tampa;* ARTHUR J. LEWIS, *University of Florida, Gainesville;* JEAN MARANI, *Communications Consultant, Tallahassee*

Georgia:
GERALD FIRTH, *University of Georgia, Athens;* LOUISE McCOMMONS, *CSRA/CESA, Thompson;* ROSS MILLER, *West Georgia College, Carrollton*

Hawaii:
FRANK B. BROWN, *University of Hawaii, Honolulu;* ANN PORT, *Hawaii Department of Education, Honolulu*

Idaho:
RICHARD L. HART, *Boise State University, Boise;* DAVID A. CARROLL, *Public Schools, Boise*

Illinois:
ALLAN DORNSEIF, *Public Schools, Matteson;* CHET DUGGAR, *Public Schools, Peoria;* MARY ANNE ELSON, *Public Schools, Springfield;* RICHARD HANKE, *Public Schools, Arlington Heights;* KATHRYN RANSOM, *Reading Coordinator, Springfield;* SYBIL YASTROW, *Public Schools, Waukegan*

Indiana:
RICHARD FLATT, *Public Schools, New Albany;* DONNA DELPH, *Purdue University Calumet Campus, Hammond;* M. SUE PIFER, *Public Schools, Columbus*

Iowa:
ELAINE McNALLY JARCHOW, *Iowa State University, Ames;* BETTY ATWOOD, *Public Schools, Ankenny;* LUTHER KISER, *Public Schools, Ames*

Kansas:
GERALD D. BAILEY, *Kansas State University, Manhattan;* JAMES JARRETT, *Public Schools, Kansas City;* GLENN PYLE, *Public Schools, McPherson*

Kentucky:
JUDY MINNEHAN, *Public Schools, LaGrange;* JACK NEEL, *Western Kentucky University, Bowling Green;* THOMAS TAYLOR, *Public Schools, Owenton*

Louisiana:
JAMES E. KENNISON, *Public Schools, New Roads;* CATHERINE JANES, *Public Schools, Lafayette;* KATE SCULLY, *Public Schools, Kenner*

Maine:

JOHN FORTIER, *Public Schools, Danforth;* RICHARD BABB, *Public Schools, Auburn*

Maryland:

DOROTHY T. CAVENEE, *Frederick County Public Schools (Retired), Frederick;* JANICE WICKLESS, *State Department of Education, Baltimore;* DENNIS YOUNGER, *Public Schools, Annapolis*

Massachusetts:

GILBERT BULLEY, *Public Schools, Lynnfield;* PAUL U. CONGDEN, *Springfield College, Springfield;* ROBERT MUNNELLY, *Public Schools, Reading;* C. BURLEIGH WELLINGTON, *Tufts University, Medford*

Michigan:

RITA M. FOOTE, *Public Schools, Southfield;* DAVID NEWBURY, *Public Schools, Hazel Park;* STUART RANKIN, *Public Schools, Detroit;* PHIL ROBINSON, *Public Schools, River Rouge;* VIRGINIA SORENSON, *Western Michigan University, Kalamazoo;* GEORGE WOONS, *Public Schools, Grand Rapids*

Minnesota:

KAREN JOHNSON, *Public Schools, St. Paul;* THOMAS MYHRA, *Public Schools, Fridley;* ARNOLD W. NESS, *Public Schools, Minneapolis*

Mississippi:

BOBBI COLLUM, *Public Schools, Jackson;* MILDRED WILLIAMS, *State Department of Education, Jackson*

Missouri:

PAUL N. FREDSTROM, *Public Schools, Webster Groves;* FRANK MORLEY, *Public Schools, Ladue;* ANNE PRICE, *Public Schools, St. Louis*

Montana:

LEROY CASAGRANDE, *Montana State University, Bozeman;* DONALD R. WALDRON, *Public Schools, Libby*

Nebraska:

LARRY L. DLUGOSH, *Public Schools, Elkhorn;* EDGAR A. KELLEY, *University of Nebraska, Lincoln;* MARLIN NELSON, *Public Schools, Ralston*

Nevada:

BRUCE MILLER, *Public Schools, Las Vegas;* MELVIN KIRCHNER, *Public Schools, Washoe County School District, Reno*

New Hampshire:

JOHN ROBERTSON, *Public Schools, Exeter;* FRED KING, *Public Schools, Exeter*

New Jersey:

MARIAN LEIBOWITZ, *Education Consultant, Lawrenceville;* PAUL BRAUNGART, *Public Schools, Moorestown;* WILLIAM CUFF, *Public Schools, Chat-*

ham; FRANK JAGGARD, *Public Schools, Cinnaminson;* WILLIAM KIEVIT, *Public Schools, Moorestown*

New Mexico:

DELBERT C. DYCHE, *Public Schools, Las Cruces;* ZEE HUNTER, *Public Schools, Roswell*

New York:

MARCIA KNOLL, *Public Schools, Forest Hills;* THOMAS CURTIS, *State University of New York, Albany;* ANTHONY DEIULIO, *State University College at Fredonia, Fredonia;* STEPHEN B. FISHER, *Public Schools, Mt. Kisco;* DOROTHY FOLEY, *State Education Department, Albany;* TIMOTHY M. MELCHIOR, *Public Schools, Valley Stream;* MILDRED NESS, *Public Schools, Rochester;* ROBERT SMITH, *Public Schools, Cedarhurst*

North Carolina:

MARY HELEN SPELLER, *Public Schools, Laurinburg;* LUCILLE BAZEMORE, *Public Schools, Windsor;* ROBERT C. HANES, *Charlotte/Mecklenburg Public Schools, Charlotte;* MARCUS C. SMITH, *Public Schools, Salisbury*

North Dakota:

FREDERICK E. PETERSON, *University of North Dakota, Grand Forks;* QUINN BRUNSON, *University of North Dakota, Grand Forks*

Ohio:

ROBERT J. HOHMAN, *Public Schools, Avon Lake;* MICHAEL BARNHART, *Public Schools, Troy;* ROBERT BENNETT, *Public Schools, Gahanna;* EUGENE GLICK, *Public Schools (Retired), Medina;* ISOBEL PFEIFFER, *University of Akron, Akron*

Oklahoma:

ROSA BELLE HESS, *Public Schools, Tulsa;* JAMES ROBERTS, *Public Schools, Lawton;* NELDA TEBOW, *Public Schools, Oklahoma City*

Oregon:

MATTHEW DOHERTY, *Public Schools, Lexington;* DON EMBERLIN, *Public Schools, Milwaukee;* REA M. JANES, *Public Schools, Portland*

Pennsylvania:

DAVID CAMPBELL, *State Department of Education, Harrisburg;* JOSEPH KANE, *Tarleton School, Devon;* ANTHONY LABRIOLA, *Tuscarora Intermediate Unit, McVeytown;* JEANNE N. ZIMMERMAN, *Public Schools (Retired), Millersville*

Puerto Rico:

RAMON CLAUDIO-TIRADO, *University of Puerto Rico, San Juan;* LILLIAN RAMOS, *Catholic University, Ponce*

Rhode Island:

NORA WALKER, *Public Schools, Warwick;* GUY N. DIBIASIO, *Public Schools, Cranston*

South Carolina:
JAMES WILHIDE, *State Department of Education, Columbia;* MILTON
KIMPSON, *State Health, Education, and Human Services, Columbia;*
CECIL WARD, *Public Schools, Florence*
South Dakota:
DELILA CASELLI, *Public Schools, Sioux Falls;* PHIL VIK, *Public Schools,
Vermillion*
Tennessee:
EVERETTE E. SAMS, *Middle Tennessee State University, Murfreesboro;*
ELIZABETH R. LANE, *Public Schools, Memphis;* JOHN LOVELL, *University
of Tennessee, Knoxville*
Texas:
GERI STRADER, *Public Schools, Houston;* ROBERT ANDERSON, *Texas Tech-
nological University, Lubbock;* M. GEORGE BOWDEN, *Public Schools
(Retired), Austin;* EDWARD CLINE, *Public Schools, Houston;* DEWEY
MAYS, *Public Schools (Retired), Fort Worth*
Utah:
C. MORGAN HAWKES, *Public Schools, Brigham City;* FLORENCE BARTON,
Weber State College, Kaysville
Vermont:
JAMES FITZPATRICK, *Public Schools, Hinesburg;* LARRY KETCHAM, *Public
Schools, Charlotte*
Virginia:
MICHAEL DeNOIA, *Public Schools, Charles City;* EVELYN BICKHAM, *Lynch-
burg College, Lynchburg;* CLARK DOBSON, *George Mason University, Fair-
fax;* DELORES GREEN, *Public Schools, Richmond*
Washington:
CONNIE KRAVIS, *Washington State University, Pullman;* FRANCIS HUNKINS,
University of Washington, Seattle; MONICA SCHMIDT, *Department of
Public Instruction, Olympia*
West Virginia:
ANN SHELLY, *Bethany College, Bethany;* HELEN SAUNDERS, *State Depart-
ment of Education, Charleston*
Wisconsin:
MARY ANN ALLEN, *Public Schools, Middleton;* LEROY McGARY, *Public
Schools, Menomonie;* RUSSELL MOSELY, *State Department of Public In-
struction, Madison*
Wyoming:
DONNA CONNOR, *University of Wyoming Field Representative, Rawling;*
CHARLENE STOGSDILL, *Public Schools, Cheyenne*

ASCD Review Council

Chairperson: HAROLD G. SHANE, *University Professor of Education, Indiana University, Bloomington*

DELMO DELLA-DORA, *Professor and Chairperson, Department of Teacher Education, California State University, Hayward*

CHARLES KINGSTON, *Principal, Thomas Fowler Junior High School, Tigard, Oregon*

GLENYS UNRUH, *Public Schools (Retired), Clayton, Missouri*

ASCD Headquarters Staff

ASCD Publications, Spring 1981

Yearbooks

A New Look at Progressive Education
(610-17812) $8.00
Considered Action for Curriculum Improvement
(610-80186) $9.75
Education for an Open Society
(610-74012) $8.00
Evaluation as Feedback and Guide
(610-17700) $6.50
Feeling, Valuing, and the Art of Growing:
Insights into the Affective
(610-77104) $9.75
Life Skills in School and Society
(610-17786) $5.50
Lifelong Learning—A Human Agenda
(610-79160) $9.75
Perceiving, Behaving, Becoming: A New Focus
for Education   (610-17278) $5.00
Perspectives on Curriculum Development
1776-1976   (610-76078) $9.50
Schools in Search of Meaning
(610-75044) $8.50
Staff Development/Organization Development
(610-81232) $9.75

Books and Booklets

About Learning Materials   (611-78134) $4.50
Action Learning: Student Community Service
Projects   (611-74018) $2.50
Adventuring, Mastering, Associating: New
Strategies for Teaching Children
(611-76080) $5.00
Approaches to Individualized Education
(611-80204) $4.75
Bilingual Education for Latinos
(611-78142) $6.75
Classroom-Relevant Research in the Language
Arts   (611-78140) $7.50
Clinical Supervision—A State of the Art Review
(611-80194) $3.75
Curricular Concerns in a Revolutionary Era
(611-17852) $6.00
Curriculum Leaders: Improving Their Influence
(611-76084) $4.00
Curriculum Materials 1980   (611-80198) $3.00
Curriculum Theory   (611-77112) $7.00
Degrading the Grading Myths: A Primer of
Alternatives to Grades and Marks
(611-76082) $6.00
Educating English-Speaking Hispanics
(611-80202) $6.50
Elementary School Mathematics: A Guide to
Current Research   (611-75056) $5.00
Eliminating Ethnic Bias in Instructional
Materials: Comment and Bibliography
(611-74020) $3.25
Global Studies: Problems and Promises for
Elementary Teachers   (611-76086) $4.50
Handbook of Basic Citizenship Competencies
(611-80196) $4.75
Humanistic Education: Objectives and
Assessment   (611-78136) $4.75
Learning More About Learning
(611-17310) $2.00
Measuring and Attaining the Goals of Education
(611-80210) $6.50

Middle School in the Making
(611-74024) $5.00
The Middle School We Need
(611-75060) $2.50
Moving Toward Self-Directed Learning
(611-79166) $4.75
Multicultural Education: Commitments, Issues,
and Applications   (611-77108) $7.00
Needs Assessment: A Focus for Curriculum
Development   (611-75048) $4.00
Observational Methods in the Classroom
(611-17948) $3.50
Open Education: Critique and Assessment
(611-75054) $4.75
Partners: Parents and Schools
(611-79168) $4.75
Professional Supervision for Professional
Teachers   (611-75046) $4.50
Reschooling Society: A Conceptual Model
(611-17950) $2.00
The School of the Future—NOW
(611-17920) $3.75
Schools Become Accountable: A PACT
Approach   (611-74016) $3.50
The School's Role as Moral Authority
(611-77110) $4.50
Selecting Learning Experiences: Linking
Theory and Practice   (611-78138) $4.75
Social Studies for the Evolving Individual
(611-17952) $3.00
Staff Development: Staff Liberation
(611-77106) $6.50
Supervision: Emerging Profession
(611-77796) $5.00
Supervision in a New Key   (611-17926) $2.50
Urban Education: The City as a Living
Curriculum   (611-80206) $6.50
What Are the Sources of the Curriculum?
(611-17522) $1.50
Vitalizing the High School   (611-74026) $3.50
Developmental Characteristics of Children and
Youth (wall chart)   (611-75058) $2.00

**Discounts on quantity orders of same title to
single address: 10-49 copies, 10%; 50 or more
copies, 15%. Make checks or money orders
payable to ASCD. Orders totaling $20.00 or
less must be prepaid. Orders from institutions
and businesses must be on official purchase
order form. Shipping and handling charges will
be added to billed purchase orders.** *Please be
sure to list the stock number of each publication, shown in parentheses.*

Subscription to *Educational Leadership*—**$18.00
a year. ASCD Membership dues: Regular (subscription [$18] and yearbook)—$34.00 a year;
Comprehensive (includes subscription [$18]
and yearbook plus other books and booklets
distributed during period of membership)—
$44.00 a year.**

Order from:

**Association for Supervision and
Curriculum Development
225 North Washington Street
Alexandria, Virginia 22314**